THE
BIRD'S
SONG

TIMOTHY M. BURKE

ISBN: 0615850766
ISBN 13: 9780615850764

Library of Congress Control Number: 2013913209
CreateSpace Independent Publishing Platform
North Charleston, South Carolina

TABLE OF CONTENTS

This is a true story. Though I have chosen to present it much like a novel, written in third person and with myself as a "character" in the book, the events of this story are nonfiction. Several of the names of the characters in this book have been changed to protect their identities, including some police officers, the victims of crimes as well as the doctors who provided medical treatment. Many of the court-room scenes are taken directly from transcripts and police reports, while other conversations and dialogue are from memory. All the places mentioned in the book are actual locations set in and around America's greatest city.

Finally, I would like to thank my friend Ruth as well as all of the women in my life who have taught me that nothing in life is random.

—Timothy M. Burke

PROLOGUE

Beacon Hill is a square mile of stately brownstones and Federal-style row houses occupied by some of the wealthiest citizens in the Commonwealth of Massachusetts. Narrow brick sidewalks and cobblestone streets illuminated by gas lanterns transport modern-day visitors to another time and place, 150 years into the recesses of the past.

Bordered by the Massachusetts State House, the Public Garden, and Boston Common, the summit once hosted a navigational beacon for ships at sea. Named after the guiding light from the tower high above the surrounding landscape, Beacon Hill was excavated in the early 1830s. The top seventy feet of the three peaks were used as landfill in a nearby marshy area known as Mill Pond. For years, horse-drawn carts and local box trains toiled night and day to transport the rocks and loam from Beacon Hill to fill in the nearby mosquito-infested swamp. When completed, the project added fifty acres to Boston proper and created a new landscape named Pemberton Square.

Nearly one hundred years later, in 1937, the "new" Suffolk County Courthouse was completed in Pemberton Square on top of the land excavated from Beacon Hill. Construction of the courthouse took over four years under a federal works project begun by Franklin Delano Roosevelt during the Great Depression. The building brought with it the promise of justice for those crossing its threshold.

For a decade beginning in the early 1980s, the courthouse would become the focal point of the intertwining cases of three women and their lawyer, four lives connected by a common bond of tragedy: random hearts, struggling against a loss of faith.

This is their story.

PRINCE OF THE CITY

Percolating with the anxious twitch of a thoroughbred at Suffolk Downs, the detectives from the drug unit hunkered down in their seats to avoid detection. There were five of them in three unmarked cars parked at the intersection of Ashmont and Adams Streets, waiting. The group took turns looking at their watches and then scanning the oncoming traffic that was slowly winding down the rain-slick street toward them.

"You think the piece of shit will show?" one of them asked his partner as he flipped the radio dial in search of the Red Sox game.

"Yeah, he'll show. It's the greed factor. The 'Prince' knows there's a score to be made. He's looking at doubling, maybe even tripling his money from the kilo after he cuts it up."

"We got the search warrant for his house too, right?"

"Yeah, it's all set."

An assistant clerk at the Dorchester District Court had issued the search warrant earlier that afternoon. The warrant authorized the search of the premises at 192 Neponset Avenue, a nondescript two-family house in a blue-collar, working-class neighborhood in Dorchester.

Lawrence E. "Larry" Goldman was an accomplished drug dealer, police informant, restaurant owner, and together with his pleasant wife Ellen, were the current occupants of the first-floor apartment at the same Neponset Avenue address. Goldman's home was the target listed in the warrant issued to search for a "large quantity of cocaine."

Beyond redemption, Goldman was a slick-talking, serpentine-chained career criminal who, years earlier, had turned informant in a high-profile case involving the murder and armed robbery of an elderly couple in the affluent city of Newton, Massachusetts. Goldman's testimony convicted cohorts Robert Stewart and James Doherty, and got Goldman a free pass for his role in that murder and for a second incident involving the shooting of a local police officer.

Shortly after Stewart and Doherty's convictions for second-degree murder, Goldman was paroled and released into society, seemingly immune from prosecution. He carried himself with a swagger of arrogance, an aura of impunity, free to break whatever laws he chose without fear of retribution. Goldman was an upscale felon with entrenched connections on both sides of the law. Upwardly mobile in the drug trade, he eventually graduated to multi-kilo buys, unfettered by the laws of ordinary men.

Frustrated by his success, some cops took to calling him the "Prince of the City."

On the evening of September 14, 1978, the Prince of the City was stopped by five members of the Boston police drug unit while in his car at the corner of Ashmont and Adams. They pulled him out at gunpoint and later discovered $12,224 in cash inside his car.

"You goin' down tonight, motherfucker," one of the cops said as he nestled the barrel of his revolver under Goldman's chin.

"We'll see about that." The Prince of the City smiled just before the right side of his pockmarked face hit the smooth metal surface of the hood of his car.

Later that night, the drug cops discovered nearly a pound of cocaine and a snub-nose revolver inside Goldman's first-floor apartment on Neponset Avenue.

Despite the significance of the charges, Goldman was released on bail for short money the following morning.

Twenty-four hours after his arrest, Goldman made the trip back to Boston police headquarters at 154 Berkeley Street. There the drug dealer accused one of the drug detectives of stealing $8,000 that he had previously hidden in a secret drawer of a shadow box hanging on the living room wall of his Dorchester apartment.

It would be the first time in twenty-five years that a Boston police officer had ever been charged with a felony.

FENWAY PARK

For decades, being a fan of the Boston Red Sox was an act of faith. It required believing without knowing, praying without deliverance, and years of endless, puritanical suffering as the end of each season inexorably wound down to the timeworn mantra of "wait 'til next year."

Sixty years of broken hearts.

It was just over two weeks after Goldman's arrest, October 2, 1978, and the date of a one-game playoff between the Red Sox and the Yankees. The final game came after a monumental season that saw Boston's "Olde Towne Team" take a ten-game lead over New York in early July, only to lose their advantage in late September as the Bombers swept the Red Sox in a four-game weekend edition of the second "Boston Massacre."

The entire city was cast into a funk of despair after the dreaded Yankees took a one-game lead with only seven games remaining. For many of the locals, it was simply more of the same, a lingering inferiority complex of self-doubt that had grown and been nurtured by decades of disappointment.

The final week of the baseball season saw the Yankees win the first six, and then on October 1, lose their final game against the Cleveland Indians. Undaunted, the Red Sox won seven straight in the final week, forcing a tie for the division championship. Each team finished with identical 99–63 season records. A coin toss would decide where the playoff game would be held.

In an omen of good fortune, the Sox won the flip of the coin. Fenway Park would be the scene of one of the greatest baseball games ever to be played.

I wonder if it was a heads or tails, the young man with the worn Red Sox cap said to himself as he stood outside gate B beneath the Green Monster on Lansdowne Street.

His name was Tim Burke. He was an idealistic, small-town farm boy who first saw the Atlantic Ocean at the age of twenty-one while standing on the shores of America's greatest city. A transplanted upstate New Yorker, he came to Boston for law school and switched allegiance from the Yankees to the Red Sox after experiencing the exhilaration and heartbreak of the 1975 World Series. The Yankees represented his past, and the Red Sox, flawed as they might be, were his future.

The transformation from the rural town of his youth brought with it a range of opportunities and experiences previously unknown. There were museums, beaches, and restaurants of every stripe in his new home. People in Boston even spoke differently. The city held a magical history along with the promise of tomorrow that simultaneously blended together into the harmony of day-to-day life.

Three years after his arrival in Boston, Burke was a newly appointed assistant district attorney with no ticket to the game. He nevertheless felt the need to be at the mecca of baseball for this moment of history. The game was a chance to be a witness to a rare sports event, even if it meant standing alone outside Fenway Park listening to the roar of the crowd.

The historic contest would be played on a glorious New England autumn sixty-five-degree day with crisp linen clouds dotting the Boston skyline. Burke stood opposite the Cask and Flagon bar, as three big-bellied scalpers were poised for the opportunity to rake in huge profits from each cherished ticket clutched tightly in their hands.

"Need tickets?" they inquired quietly just out of earshot and eyesight of the nearby uniformed walking beat cops.

His eyes shifted momentarily to the street vendors hawking bags of peanuts, cashews, and pistachios in brown paper bags as the smell of grilled Italian sausages, onions, and peppers wafted and lingered in the air. Nearby, a group of fans rhythmically chanted, "Let's go, Red Sox," as thousands of others adorned with their obligatory team hats and replica uniform shirts passed down Brookline Avenue and Yawkey Way, through the turnstiles and into the lush green of Fenway. Once inside, the fans stood and roared with approval as the Red Sox players were introduced. The throng was flushed and breathless, anxious for the first pitch.

With the eventual passing of the crowd, the streets surrounding the stadium went suddenly quiet. Discarded hot dog wrappers swirled amid the crush of shucked peanut shells and leftover game-day scorecards as the throaty voice of Sherm Feller announced the leadoff hitter for the visiting team to a chorus of hometown boos.

The words, "Now batting for the New York Yankees, number seventeen, center fielder, Mickey Rivers, Rivers," echoed from inside the park out to Lansdowne Street and down Yawkey Way.

It wasn't a major incident as he recalled the moment years later, but as Burke stood near the entrance to gate B, he saw a familiar face approach the ballpark entrance. He was midthirties with a bold presence that came with years of dealing with the darker edge of life. A solitary latecomer to the start of the game, he stood impatiently waiting outside the turnstile as the elderly ticket taker raised both hands in an upward defensive motion and slowly shook his head.

Clearly, there were no tickets available. Undeterred, the man simultaneously reached for his wallet, produced a shiny gold badge, and then pushed his way past.

Burke had occasionally seen him in the crowded corridors of the courthouse where he worked. He was part of the Boston police drug unit, a specialized group of detectives, organized into squads whose citywide jurisdiction enabled them to work all of Boston. They were undercover nomads who relished the hunt of upper-level dealers in an era of widespread cocaine use.

He silently watched as the man disappeared into the shadows of the stadium, never realizing in that moment the connection the two would later share.

Over the span of the next three hours, the sounds of the game ebbed and flowed as the fans from both teams reacted to each instance of a player's success or failure. There was a pulsating rhythm to the predominately white crowd as a nearby radio provided the play-by-play as seen through the eyes of announcer Ned Martin.

In the latter innings of the game, the arc of the setting sun cast a dark shadow midway between the pitcher's mound and home plate. In right field, the unrelenting glare of sunlight blinded players from both teams.

5

A fitting end to such a historic moment would of course require the game to be decided in the final inning. Life didn't disappoint, at least up to that point. In the bottom of the ninth inning, the Red Sox trailed five to four with two outs, but with the tying run standing at third base. There was a hush of anticipation as Carl Yastrzemski strode toward home plate.

Burke felt an unconscious connection with the man who wore the number 8 on his uniform. Maybe it was because both had been raised in small farming communities in New York and somehow made the transition to life in Boston. Whatever the reason, "Yaz" had become the beating heart of the Red Sox. He was the one certainty in a world of uncertainty. He was the captain of the team who always made the miraculous play, the clutch hit, the game-saving catch braced against the Green Monster where he patrolled left field.

The air hung heavy as Yaz slowly raised his bat above the level of his shoulders, and each Red Sox fan collectively prayed for a hit, a wild pitch, or an error—anything to tie the score.

The large right-hander on the mound stared in at his catcher, and within seconds the ball flashed from the pitcher's hand. The nearly simultaneous sound of Yaz's bat making contact was lost in the sudden roar of the crowd. The white orb soared upward and momentarily held the hopes of thousands of fans in the balance. The ball peaked, glimmered in the fading sunlight, drifted left, and then quickly fell back to earth into the soft leather webbing of the Yankee third baseman's glove.

"Maybe they'll win it all next year," Burke said aloud to no one in particular.

NEWMAN'S MEAT LAND

Newman's Meat Land was a small neighborhood market in the insular city of Chelsea, Massachusetts. An urban suburb of Boston, Chelsea was a melting pot of ethnicity and religion for its thirty thousand residents. It was a poor city, where single mothers headed almost a quarter of the households. Located near Broadway Street, barely two blocks beneath the shadow of the monstrous Tobin Bridge, the store was the de facto center of local politics and neighborhood affairs for three decades.

David Newman was the owner of Newman's Meat Land and the descendant of a Jewish immigrant who drove a horse-drawn ice wagon through the streets of Chelsea. Newman married a local woman, had two children, and settled into a comfortable existence across the Mystic River, four miles from the center of Boston. Although he dearly loved his community, the elder Newman wanted better for his only son, Mark.

Burke met Mark Newman on a clear Indian summer day. The younger Newman was cerebral, with a disarming smile and curly brown hair. They would become lifelong friends. Both had recently graduated from law school and been hired by the Suffolk County District Attorney's Office to prosecute cases in the chaos of the district courts surrounding Boston. The salary was ten grand for the year.

The newly admitted lawyers were the same height, weight, and age, one Catholic, the other Jewish. They shared a mutual love of sports as well as the law, with each day bringing another opportunity to revel in both their cases and the local teams before court began.

A stone wall fronting the aging courthouse was the frequent outdoor lunch spot for the two assistant district attorneys making short work of the contents of their brown bag lunches.

"How'd your trial go this morning?" Burke began as the early afternoon sun warmed the conversation.

There was a measure of wry humor and self-deprecation to the lawyer from Chelsea, who for some reason always referred to his friend by his proper first name.

"Not so great, Timothy. I asked my first witness what his *avocation* was after he was sworn in. He looked at me kind of strangely and told me he usually took off the first two weeks in August. The judge cracked up, and so did the clerk and everyone else in the courtroom. How about you?"

"I got a call this morning from Mr. Leary, the first assistant. He asked me to interview some witnesses on a case the Boston police have been investigating for the past couple of weeks. It's a cocaine dealer who claims one of the guys from the drug unit stole some money during a search at his house in Dorchester."

"Yeah, I remember reading about that case in the newspapers."

"The dealer's name is Larry Goldman. He claims one of the detectives stole a wad of hundred-dollar bills hidden in some kind of knickknack shelf in his apartment."

Newman listened intently, but said nothing as his companion continued.

"It's funny, where I grew up there weren't any drugs or violence like there is here. It's all kind of new to me," Burke explained to his friend.

"It was just the opposite for me in Chelsea. I've seen firsthand what drugs can do to people. The broken lives, the misery it causes, the destruction of entire neighborhoods. In a strange way, Newman's Meat Land was like a safe haven for people in Chelsea. After my father died, things changed dramatically all around the block. We sold the store and I made my mother and sister move out. It just was never the same anymore. I feel like the same thing is happening in Dorchester."

Burke studied Newman's expression before responding.

"I think I know what you mean. Anyway, I interviewed the witnesses this morning. Goldman came in with his attorney, his wife, Ellen, and her sister. Goldman's a real sleaze, but his wife and her sister seem very nice."

"What's the detective's name he says took the money?"

"Frost. Al Frost."

"You realize, Timothy, if you prove Frost stole the money, Goldman will probably walk on the drug charges?"

8

"Yeah, I know."

"So how'd the interviews go?"

"Well, it's kind of straightforward. Goldman's sister-in-law is the only one who says she saw the detective take the money from the shadow box and put it in his pocket. Her name's Mary O'Donnell. She's a nursing student at Boston City Hospital."

"Do you believe her?" Newman asked as a small furrow creased the eyebrows hidden behind his horn-rimmed glasses.

FROST

It was easy to like Al Frost. He smiled often, spoke softly, and had a presence that evoked the feeling of ready comfort. Recently divorced, Frost was of average height, with thinning sandy-colored hair, a barrel chest, and deep-set dark brown eyes.

The investigation of the Frost case consumed Burke for more than a year. Goldman's allegations spawned additional claims of theft of drug money from other drug dealers in the Boston area. There were recurring rumors of lax supervision and case manipulation, with allegations of informants buying their way out of prison sentences in exchange for providing marginal information and, more important, remaining silent about stolen drug money. Burke interviewed known dealers, cops, defense attorneys, and judges about what they knew and were willing to talk about. He reviewed every search warrant and drug conviction for the past five years for clues.

In the end, Burke came away convinced the vast majority of detectives in the drug unit were honest cops, but equally certain that others had taken advantage of opportunities to enrich themselves. He communicated each day with Newman about his feelings and what the evidence showed.

"You're taking on a culture of acceptance in the police department of the way things are. That's never easy. Just get the facts out. The best disinfectant is sunshine," his friend told him.

Fanned by the news media, the Frost case created significant friction between the DA's office and the BPD, with the rank and file of police supporting the popular detective. There was good reason to do so. Goldman was a known dealer with a reputation for far worse than selling cocaine. No one openly condoned stealing money from a drug dealer, but there were worse things in the minds of many. In his heart Burke knew Mary

O'Donnell was telling the truth and that he was doing the right thing, but persuading a jury to accept her testimony would be another story.

The trial *de novo* system in place in Massachusetts at the time allowed a defendant the chance to have two trials for the same offense. The first before a judge without a jury and then, if convicted, permitted an appeal for a second trial before a jury of eight citizens. In an acrimonious first trial before District Court Judge Arthur Sherman, detective Alton Frost was convicted of the larceny of $8,000 from the shadow box in Goldman's apartment.

It would be a short-term victory.

Frost's attorney, Thomas Troy, promptly appealed the conviction and persuaded the court to postpone the imposition of his client's sentence to the House of Correction until the conclusion of his second trial.

"You just do your best and then let the chips fall where they may," Mr. Leary, the second in charge of the district attorney's office, told the younger lawyer shortly before Frost's jury trial.

Jury selection for the second Frost trial was scheduled to take place on January 7, 1980, in a cavernous courtroom on the third floor of the courthouse at Pemberton Square. Burke's first son was born at 8:27 that morning. The judge postponed empanelment until the next day.

The trial would last three weeks.

Like a character written out of a Damon Runyon novel, Frost's lawyer was an Irish warrior and former marine in his early fifties. Armed with a quick wit, a ruddy complexion, and a two-fisted pugilist's approach to the trial of cases, Tom Troy relished his role as the defender of the underdog from the forces of perceived evil. The son of a Boston police detective, Troy was born two weeks after his father was shot and killed while making an arrest of a suspect in Boston's South End.

Frost's second trial was a raucous carnival with full audience participation. Troy's cross-examination of Goldman was eminently predictable and equally effective.

The defense attorney exploited his adversary on the stand as a drug-and-death-dealing hardcore criminal who stood to benefit from the claim of theft made against his undeserving client. "If anyone should be sitting in the defendant's chair, it's the Gold Man," Frost's lawyer roared to the jury as the packed audience of the detective's friends and supporters nodded and audibly mumbled in agreement.

The road wasn't as smooth with Mary O'Donnell. She stood her ground despite Troy's withering attempts to undermine the credibility of what she had seen his client do. Despite Troy's best efforts, there was no shaking her testimony. The jury had been amused by the body shots to the Commonwealth's case before Mary O'Donnell took the stand, but sobered quickly by the stark reality of corruption when she stepped down.

The trial roiled out of control on each successive day with charges and counterclaims from both sides. Like a runaway freight train, it was great theater, a rollicking steam engine careening down a straightway full-throttle with certain disaster ahead, but with those in attendance unable to avert their eyes from the impending crash. The media provided daily coverage that superheated the courtroom, increasing the tension between both side's perception of good versus evil.

Frost's supervisor in the drug unit, Lieutenant Henry Earl, was one of the last witnesses called to the stand. A pleasant-appearing gentleman, Earl oozed sincerity and spoke with a deep, gravelly voice. After a few preliminary questions, Earl was asked by Troy whether he personally believed Frost was innocent of taking the money from the shadow box. Burke knew he should object. He quickly placed his hands on the arms of his chair to stand and speak, but he hesitated long enough for the answer to be given, and in that moment, he feared the case was lost.

"Yes, I think he's innocent," the witness told the jury as a rush of blood and dread rose throughout Burke's body.

The jury would return with their decision late the following night.

There was a blur of sounds and thoughts as Burke stared straight ahead, waiting for the foreman to announce the jury's decision. It was as though he was stuck knee-deep in cement with clouds of drifting fog enveloping his body and eventually his mind.

"Have you reached a verdict?" the clerk asked the assembled group of jurors as the courtroom drew a silent collective breath.

"Yes, we have. We find the defendant not guilty," the voice to Burke's right side calmly stated as the courtroom erupted in extended applause, cheers, and shouts of approval from the rows of spectators seated behind the two attorneys' tables.

The jeers, curses, and taunts from the gallery echoed throughout the courtroom and seemed to grow in intensity as the seconds wore on. Burke pushed back from the prosecutor's table following the reading of the verdict and then turned to face the angry faces on both sides of the aisle separating the packed rows of the defendant's supporters. There were no bangs from the judge's gavel to silence the crowd and restore order. The judge seemed to revel in the roar of the spectators, who in turn took their cue from the bench.

Burke walked the gauntlet, absorbed the abuse, and continued to stare straight ahead as he passed each row of Frost supporters. In the last row, a silent figure stood motionless while the others surrounding him gestured and cheered. Unlike the others, the detective's hands were clasped together in front of his torso as he stood without expression and watched while the prosecutor walked slowly past.

His name was Reggie Rose.

Burke left the courtroom defeated, shamed by his failure. For some reason, his mind drifted back to Fenway Park and Carl Yastrzemski as he slowly made his way alone to the bank of courthouse elevators.

49 REVERE STREET

At 49 Revere Street, a four-story brick row house apartment building stood in a quiet, trendy section of Beacon Hill. Named after silversmith and famed equestrian Paul Revere, the cobblestone street ran perpendicular to the banks of the Charles River. The fourth floor contained a three-bedroom offering shared by a trio of friends from the Midwest who had recently moved to the East Coast in search of their careers.

The three young women never knew their new home had been the scene of an unreported rape in the fall of 1978.

The rapist was never identified or charged. He would return to the same apartment at 49 Revere Street five years later.

It was a Saturday, the last day in April 1983, and the start of another Red Sox season of failed promise. The group Toto's song "Africa" topped the charts as the hint of summer and the smell of the surf breaking along the shoreline of Boston's inner harbor wafted up State Street toward Beacon Hill and the golden dome of the capital city.

The night was still, and the cover of darkness shrouded the stranger as he stood beneath the rust-encrusted fire escape. He looked upward beyond the peak of the apartment roof cornice to the distant stars and then back. A rush of excitement coupled with desire overcame his fear of returning to prison. It made no difference in the moment. He knew what he needed as he placed his hands inside the front pockets of his jeans. There was no turning back now. The man quickly surveyed the scene around him, casually glanced upward again, and made his plan.

Rape is a particularly ugly word.

It conjures up all forms of evil in a brutal struggle of the powerful over the powerless. No matter what sordid motive drives it, be it the need for control, dominance, or feelings of rejection, the crime of rape is one of the worst things that can happen to a human being. There are those who would say it is the worst crime and wished they had died the day they were raped.

Holly Robins was one of those women.

AMADEUS

Wolfgang Mozart was an eighteenth-century genius composer of over six hundred classical works of incomparable beauty. A child prodigy mired in the throes of financial insecurity and paternal conflict, he died prematurely at the age of thirty-five, struggling to complete the composition of a requiem for his own funeral.

"Amadeus" was a pseudonym frequently used by Mozart, roughly translated to mean "the love of God." Vulgar and uncouth in his youth, Mozart became a Freemason later in life, vowing his belief in a supreme being and the betterment of humanity. Many of his subsequent compositions, such as the opera *The Magic Flute*, reflected a humanistic view of life and the tenets of innocence and joy. In his fanciful opera, the magic flute is employed to change the evil in men's hearts.

Nearly two hundred years later, a stylized stage play written about the conflicting lives of Mozart and competitor composer Antonio Salieri was playing to sold-out crowds in the theater district of Boston. The name of the play was *Amadeus.*

Holly Robins loved the theater.

The Shubert Theater is located on the lower end of Tremont Street, and at the time bordered by the "combat zone," in the midst of the city's shrinking adult entertainment area. The Shubert was known as the "Little Princess" of Boston's theaters, and it had hosted scores of productions since it was opened in January of 1910. For decades, audiences packed the sixteen-hundred-seat theater to witness performances ranging from Charlie Chaplin to Shakespeare's *Hamlet.*

The young woman from the Midwest heard the television ads about the upcoming play and told one of her roommates, who anxiously bought two tickets to *Amadeus*, placing them on the rickety nightstand beside her bed. For weeks, each night before she fell asleep, Holly closed her eyes and wondered what role in *Amadeus* she would be best suited to play.

She envisioned herself gliding across the stage with the audience in awe of her graceful movements while the power of Mozart's music lifted and guided her. There was a sensuous quality to his music that calmed and at the same time moved her.

The weather was unusually warm on the evening of April 30. The promise of summer was held within the soft night air. Holly liked her new apartment. In many ways it symbolized her independence. She felt safe there, on the fourth floor, even when she was alone. Her two roommates were out for the evening that Saturday. Holly declined their offer to join them, deciding to stay home and read before bed.

In her mind, she could hear the faint notes of Mozart mixing with a cautious creak coming from the kitchen window. The noise passed quickly as she gradually began to drift into sleep.

It must be the wind, she told herself just before the solitary figure passed silently through the frame of her bedroom door. The stranger momentarily paused and stood above her like a calculating bird of prey. The man waited for his eyes to fully adjust to the dark, patiently surveying the scene around him. The intruder eventually directed his attention toward his victim, now asleep, unaware of his presence as he stared at her body. His eyes slowly passed over the outline of her shoulders down to the curve of her waist and then the swell of her hips.

Unseen, the man reached with his right hand toward a nightstand where the tickets to *Amadeus* lay next to the alarm clock. The rapist snatched his trophy up and carefully placed the tickets in the right rear pocket of his pants. He then disconnected the phone and removed the cord to tie Holly's hands in front of her. The man grabbed a blouse to momentarily cover his face, preventing any positive identification, and then quickly wrapped it around the young woman's eyes.

Three hours later, Holly Robins sat on a gurney in the emergency room at the Tufts New England Medical Center. Her hair was matted with blood and her face beaten, unrecognizable. Streaks of tears streamed from her swollen eyes past the deep purple bruise tracing her jawline down to the two narrow red claw marks encircling her neck.

The protocol for the investigation of rape cases in the early eighties varied within every police department. Each depended upon the cooperation and trust of the victim.

The detective from the Boston police entered the emergency room with a quiet efficiency, patiently standing in front of the young woman, waiting for the right moment to speak. Holly's head was bowed, and her hands trembled as he gently took her hand in his own.

Reggie Rose sensed the victim somehow felt ashamed, refusing to raise her head as he slowly began to speak.

"It's not your fault," he told her, noticing the young woman didn't pull her hand away from his touch.

Holly moved her head from side to side in silent response without looking up.

The detective knelt down on one knee below her line of sight to make eye contact with the young woman's blank gaze.

"We're gonna catch this guy, OK? You and me, we're going to do this together. We're gonna find out who did this to you, I promise, OK?" he vowed, slowly beginning the process of empowerment.

Rose didn't ask any questions that night. He didn't want the young woman to have to repeat the horror more times than she needed to. He looked at her face, disfigured from the beating, and spoke what words of comfort his mind would allow, hiding his own sense of rage.

When she did begin to talk, it was with a halting rasp.

"I-I can't talk to you alone. I want my dad to be with me," Holly told the detective with the dark, intense eyes.

"Whatever you need, we're going to do," Rose told her. "How about tomorrow?"

There was a fragmented pause before Holly spoke again. It was as if she was gathering strength, just enough to think about the next day.

"I called my father. My family's flying here from home to be with me. I feel so bad. I never heard my dad cry before," Holly said softly as she slowly raised her eyes for the first time.

Nearby, the warm breeze ebbed down Revere Street in the early morning air, lingering momentarily with the promise that came with another sunrise. Overhead, a flock of sleek Canada geese traced the curve of the Atlantic, en route to a small inlet south of Ellsworth, Maine.

AREA A

The Boston Police Department is the oldest in the country, originating from a night watch patrol of six unpaid officers dating back to the early 1630s. In more recent times, the department had grown to over two thousand sworn officers. The city's current geographic patrols were divided into five separate areas, identified by the first five letters of the alphabet.

The headquarters of Area A is a foreboding, large, brick-and-concrete police station located on New Sudbury Street, about a block from the Suffolk County Courthouse in Pemberton Square. Area A's jurisdiction encompasses most of downtown Boston, from Copley Square to Charlestown, through the Callahan Tunnel to East Boston and back to Faneuil Hall and Beacon Hill. Many of the city's major perps are funneled through the front doors of the squat edifice adjoining nearby Channel 7. The detective division took up almost the entire fourth floor.

The large man and his daughter were shown into the unadorned reception area of Area A late the next morning and then directed to the fourth-floor interview room where the dark-eyed detective waited with a small stack of yellow notepads and matching yellow number two pencils.

The interview took over two hours and began with a series of questions about the victim and then led into an open narrative of what had happened to Holly. It was a summary of what the victim remembered about the worst moments of her life. Rose followed his normal pattern by asking questions about Holly's background, her age, marital status, education, work history, and the events leading up to the actual assault. Once the victim crossed the threshold into the description of the rape, Rose stopped asking questions and simply listened.

As Holly sat facing the detective, her father held her hand and softly began to cry during the interview. He struggled against the tears while his daughter explained the beating, her refusal to submit, being bound by the telephone cord and blinded by her blouse. She told Rose of the multiple rapes, orally, vaginally, and anally over a period of more than two hours, and how degraded the unknown man had made her feel.

As the young woman spoke, her breath came in short, labored gasps, while her father helplessly clenched and unclenched his powerful hands.

"I begged him to stop. I told him that he was hurting me, and he just kept saying, 'Honey, you don't know what pain is, but you're going to find out.'"

Holly told the detective of the seemingly never-ending punches and kicks to her body. She had prepared her mind for the final blow that would take her life. She briefly thought of her own funeral, praying that her family would be able to see her face one more time as they had always known her, explaining that she didn't want a closed casket.

"He told me to turn my head away as he stood over me. I closed my eyes and did as I was told."

She heard the stranger's footsteps as the sounds moved away from her toward the bathroom, hesitated, and then returned. She could hear his breathing as she sensed him standing over her while she lay on the ground naked, exposed. She felt him spread her legs and pour the remains of a bottle of mouthwash inside her to destroy any traceable evidence of semen. Holly could smell the familiar scent of wintergreen as she struggled help-lessly against his strength. She lost all sensation in her hands as the pressure of the cream-colored telephone cord encircling her wrists turned her fingers a cold, bloodless hue of blue.

"It's strange the different paths life takes us down. It all seems so uncon-nected, but maybe it isn't," Holly would later say to the detective when the interview was finally completed.

Rose nodded, but he didn't respond as the young woman and her father stood to leave.

At the time of Holly Robins's rape, Reggie Rose had been a police offi-cer for over ten years. He had grown accustomed to the face of crime and random violence. Like most cops, he understood the need to keep a layer of distance between himself and the victims of horrible crimes. He wasn't sure what it was that made this case so different. Why he wanted, needed, to help this stranger regain what she had lost. Maybe it was Holly's sense of innocence or her father's feelings of helplessness.

It didn't matter what the reason was.

The detective momentarily allowed the worst in him to emerge as he imagined the rapist in front of him. In his mind, Rose watched as he slowly drew his gun, placed it to the forehead of the unknown man, and without remorse, pulled the trigger. He could almost hear the sound of the discharge and feel the recoil from the gun when he heard Holly begin to speak.

"Oh, there's one other thing I almost forgot to tell you," the young woman explained.

"Sorry, what is it?" Rose asked as he returned to the moment.

"It's kind of strange, but he stole my roommate's tickets to see *Amadeus*. It's playing at the Shubert this month."

LONNIE

It was late October1983, nearly seven months after the rape of Holly Robins, and the detective from the Boston police had no suspects. For Holly, each passing day became an exercise of futility and unrelenting rage as she attempted to cope with her loss of innocence and the lack of resolution of her case.

In another part of the city and unknown to the rape victim, a frail black woman named Ruth held a tiny crucifix tightly in her right hand as she quietly entered Children's Hospital. She was holding back the flow of tears as she headed to the special care unit. The soles of her shoes made a soft swoosh as she quickly made her way to the side of her thirteen-year-old son Lonnie's bed. She could barely discern the outline of his face in the room that had been dark now for days.

Undefined anxiety had been the woman's constant companion since her son's admission, and now an avalanche of dread began to overwhelm her. Three days earlier the young boy had told his mother the lights hurt his eyes. Soon after, he drifted into a coma. Lonnie seemed to be barely breathing as his mother gently took his hand into her own.

She pressed his hand against the side of her face as she murmured, "I love you, darlin'." Her son's almond-colored skin had turned a pale tone of jaundiced yellow. Layers of fine spider-like webs of rash covered the contours of his face, swelling his eyelids into catlike slits that oozed milky-tinted pus.

"Lord, I know my life's been far from perfect, but take me instead of my Lonnie," the woman silently pleaded to a seemingly unresponsive God.

She was a woman of religion, and despite her life of faith and her prayers Ruth knew the end was near.

The boy's mother closed her eyes and thought of how she would remember her son. In her mind, she could see her Lonnie running, running with the football on that green field of grass, gliding so fast that his feet seemed to barely touch the ground. She could see him running so free, so free, with all those white boys chasing behind him, behind her Lonnie.

Outside, she could hear the faint sound of geese heading south in the night air, momentarily meshing with the rhythm of the ventilator.

The following morning, the doctors at Children's Hospital told the frail woman with the crucifix that there was nothing more they could do.

Her Lonnie was gone from her.

DEE AND SHERM

Rated as one of the top pediatric facilities in the United States, Children's Hospital was originally founded as a small twenty-two-bed medical unit in 1869. Currently located at 300 Longwood Avenue, not far from Fenway Park, the medical center had grown to its present capacity of nearly four hundred beds, employing over three thousand full-time doctors, residents, nurses, and researchers.

Deirdre and Sherman Griffiths met while both were working at Children's Hospital. They were two souls passing through the same corridors of life without a compass. Dee worked as a nurse in the intensive care unit, while Sherm was a pharmacy intern. Despite their common roots within the hospital, they were, at first blush, an unlikely pair.

She was quiet and reserved, never seeking the limelight. Sherm was Dee's mirror opposite. He was brash, self-assured, and with Dee's encouragement, he decided to leave the pharmacy at Children's to become a Boston police officer. Sherm found his career path as a detective in the drug unit and his true love in Deirdre.

Deirdre discovered a new life with Sherm. They became inseparable. The couple married, had two girls within twenty-four months, and spent their brief remaining time together in love.

On a cold, gray winter day, Sherman Griffiths was murdered when Boston police raided a drug house on Bellevue Street in Dorchester.

THE BIRD'S SONG

It was early September 1984, nearly a year after Lonnie's death at Children's Hospital and longer since the unsolved rape of Holly Robins. Shortly after the Frost trial, Burke was transferred from the district court to the homicide unit located at Pemberton Square in downtown Boston.

There was a chilly start to this Monday morning, foreboding of a harsh New England winter. Another trial was about to begin that day. The defendant's name was Antonio Gomes. He was charged with the murder of a mother and her two children on Jacobs Street in Dorchester.

Burke sat alone at the prosecution table in the barren courtroom, remembering his first day in the homicide unit. It was then that he discovered the tattered gray file containing the photographs of the woman and her two murdered children. Catalogued as "cold" and filed in a three-drawer steel cabinet, the case was already two years old when the young lawyer first discovered it. The file was a well-worn, slate-gray case jacket containing police reports, lab tests, and photographs that lured him in, shocked him, and made him want to puke with rage and horror.

The photographs told a silent story of Basilisa Melendez, a Hispanic mother of three children who had been raped and repeatedly stabbed by an unknown intruder into her home. Two of her young children hid in their bedroom, listening to their mother's screams until the killer came for them. He pulled them out separately from beneath their beds, beat them there, and then dragged them down the narrow hallway to where their mother lay dead, naked on the floor. The killer then slit the children's throats after he had stabbed them in their hearts.

Thrown against the wall where their mother lay silently waiting, the three bodies were a tangled heap of death's blood-soaked final embrace.

A crime of unspeakable violence, random and horrific, witnessed only by the eyes of the six-month-old baby left untouched in a crib not far from the family Christmas tree.

A single drop of the killer's blood was left at the crime scene. It was the only piece of evidence that could possibly link the murderer to his victims.

Once the lawyer read the file of the triple homicide, he became obsessed with finding the killer. He felt driven by an unexplainable force to solve this horrible mystery.

There was no logic to the haunting.

The triple homicide had stunned his mind and shocked his soul. Burke knew it was irrational, but he felt he was the only one who could solve the case. Each night the recurring image of the children's bodies violently and wantonly thrown against a wall by the killer dredged up a memory from the lawyer's forgotten past.

It was a dark moment from Burke's own childhood, an ominous shadow crossing the path of his life. He recalled a warm Easter Sunday when he witnessed young blackbird fledglings taken from their fallen nest by a cruel neighbor. The child in his mind remembered the large man who momentarily held the young birds helpless, powerless against his brute strength. From the bough of a tree above the older man and the young boy came the desperate sounds of the mother blackbird singing amid the thin chirping sounds of her offspring. The bird sensed the impending death of her chicks and offered the pair the only gift God had given her.

She gave the cruel man and the young boy her song.

Unmoved, the older man spoke. The boy heard his words without fully understanding their meaning.

"These birds are just like niggers. They got no reason to live," the man casually explained in a low, guttural voice.

Unable to speak, the young boy's heart beat wildly in rhythm with the trembling hearts of the captive birds. He recalled raising his hand toward the man as their mother sang above, but the man turned away, hurling their tiny bodies against a cinder block wall. The child who remained within the lawyer's mind could still recall with clarity the sounds of their bones breaking against the hardened wall.

The Gomes trial would last for nearly three weeks, with forensic experts from each side contesting the significance and identity of the drop of the killer's blood detected at the scene of the crime. After the last witness left the stand and following the attorneys' closing arguments, the judge gave the jury the instruction on reasonable doubt.

While the judge spoke, Burke studied the jurors' faces, searching for a reaction, wondering if he had convinced them, or like the Frost case, had failed.

When the instructions were done, the jury of nine women and three men retraced their steps upstairs to the cramped deliberation room above the courtroom. There they would remain and discuss the case for the next several days. From nine in the morning until five in the afternoon, the twelve citizens would wrangle over the significance of the evidence they had heard, what it all meant, who they could believe, and how it fit into the court's instructions on the law.

Downstairs there was nothing left to do but sit and wait.

The wait for the jury's decision was the worst part of a trial. The longer the deliberations continued, the more doubts the prosecutor had about what he could or should have done during the trial. There was always a question he hadn't asked on cross-examination, or one too many on direct, or something he forgot to say in his closing.

It was the process of self-doubt, driven by the fear of failure. Burke was good at it. The jury had been out for more than four days when the loud knock finally resounded from inside the door of the jury room on the eighth floor of the Suffolk County Courthouse.

They had a verdict.

There was a soft murmur of anticipation within the crowded courtroom as the spectators watched the solitary figure seated at the prosecution table. Surrounded by scores of people, he was never more alone. In many ways his life reflected the loneliness he felt at that very moment. He welcomed the finality of the case that had changed his life.

Strangely, in that moment Burke thought of the mother blackbird from the dreams of his past and, at the same time, the sheets on the children's beds. Brightly colored, they were Mickey Mouse prints with the happy Disney character welcoming the sleepy children into his open arms. The happy mouse with the four-fingered, white-gloved hands smiled at him, waving blindly from within the photographs taken of the children's vomit-and blood-soaked beds.

*****

At 11:04 that morning, the twelve solemn jurors entered the courtroom with three verdict slips clasped tightly in the forewoman's right hand.

His breath came in short, measured gasps as he closed his eyes, waiting for this moment that would define him.

"Please God, please...," Burke silently prayed as the killer behind him mimicked the same words of entreaty.

It was a mutual prayer held aloft in the undefined, delicate balance between good and evil. The lawyer wondered whose voice God would listen to that day as a desperate silence roared through his mind.

"What say you, Madam Forelady, to the indictments charging the defendant Antonio Gomes with three counts of murder in the first degree? Is he guilty or not guilty?" the clerk intoned as the crowded courtroom sat motionless, suspended in the moment.

Outside the courthouse, the autumn breeze gently turned the few remaining leaves of the maple trees on Boston Common upward to face the midday sun.

JEEPERS CREEPERS

It had been weeks since the verdict on the triple homicide.

There weren't many occasions when Burke got the call to go from his cramped quarters in room 603 to the other side of the sixth floor of the Pemberton Square courthouse where the first assistant's office was situated. The frosted-glass-paned door of Paul K. Leary was located down a long, narrow corridor made to seem even more intimidating by the lack of windows.

The second in command of the Suffolk County DA's office, Mr. Leary, as all the younger assistants knew him, sat waiting in a Gunlocke-style chair situated behind a neatly organized, glass-topped mahogany desk. He was a religious family man, with a son and three daughters and prone to using arcane phrases like "Jiminy Cricket" to spice up his day-to-day lexicon. The first assistant was also a mentor that Burke hated to disappoint.

"Come on in," Leary responded to the knock at the door.

There was a comfortable, almost paternal familiarity between the two men, born out of a shared interest in the law.

"So tell me what cases you've been working on," the older attorney said without explaining why.

"I've got two murder cases ready for trial. The first one's a young kid murdered by a Hell's Angel wannabe at a biker bar in Revere. The victim was only nineteen. He was shot in the face with birdshot from a 12-gauge Remington. The other one's a taxicab driver from Haiti. He was trying to get enough money to bring his family over here. He was shot in the head and robbed while he was on his knees begging 'em not to kill him. All he had was seven bucks in his pocket. Then I have the rape of Ginnie Freeman. It's the one from last December where the two guys kidnapped her from

Faneuil Hall. They took turns stabbing and raping her in the backseat of her car while they were driving around East Boston."

"Jeepers creepers," Leary said as his hand involuntarily covered his mouth.

"Yeah, the two of them kicked her in the head until she was unconscious. Then they threw her naked off one of the piers into the harbor and left her for dead. The water temperature that night was around fifty-five degrees. She managed to swim to shore and somebody found her," Burke stated all too matter-of-factly.

"Gawd," Leary said, wincing as if in pain. "I remember that case. She picked the two guys out of some mug shots a couple days later, right?"

"Right, she was a 'water baby.' She knew how to swim ever since she was eighteen months old. It's amazing she's still alive."

"She's willing to testify?"

"Yeah, she is."

"Sounds like you have a lot on your plate. Got room for one more?"

"Sure, what kind of case is it?"

"It's that unsolved Beacon Hill rape case one of the detectives has been working on," the first assistant explained, abruptly heading the conversation in another direction.

"You mean Reggie Rose?"

"Yeah, he's obsessed with the case and asked if we would talk to you about getting involved."

"He did? You know we've haven't spoken since the Frost case."

"I know that too, but this was a terrible rape. There's no identification because she was blindfolded the whole time. There's no suspect to compare any of the trace evidence recovered from the scene. When the cops got there, they thought they were dealing with a murder, she was beaten that badly," Leary said, measuring the response on the younger lawyer's face.

Burke briefly wondered if the first assistant's request had anything to do with Leary having three daughters and the fear that accompanies the need to protect the ones we love.

"I'll be happy to take a look at the case, but let me talk to Reggie first."

There was a pause in the conversation as Burke left his chair and took the four steps necessary to reach the frost-paned door. He wanted to tell

Mr. Leary he planned to leave the DA's office; that life had somehow changed for him, but he knew now wasn't the time.

"Oh, one other thing. I just wanted to let you know I thought you did a good job on the triple," Leary said in a monotone without elaboration as the younger lawyer left without responding.

KNUCKLEHEADS

If you caught him in a quiet moment, and there weren't many in his life, Reggie Rose would tell you he was a "knucklehead" growing up in the blue-collar city north of Boston by the name of Medford. The only people who ever pronounced Medford correctly were the ones who didn't live there. Known as "Meffah" to the locals and their relatives, Rose was a "townie," who had spent most of his life in the busy community.

Born into a strict Catholic family, Rose's father was the captain on a towboat that plied the tides of Boston Harbor. Each day, the senior Rose would haul a cavernous garbage scowl loaded with twenty-four hours' worth of the city's refuse fifteen miles out to sea, gleefully accompanied by a giddy convoy of a hundred squawking seagulls.

Another unrepentant altar boy, Reggie Rose wasn't a good student, and he didn't excel at sports. Like most kids growing up in the Boston area, Reggie loved baseball. He just wasn't any good at it. Skinny at five foot nine, with narrow, intense brown eyes, he graduated from Medford High and did two tours in Vietnam. When he came back, someone told him he would make a good detective.

It was his future wife, Donna.

"I was below average in just about everything I ever did in my life except for the woman I married and being a detective," he explained cautiously to the assistant district attorney in a rare moment of self-evaluation.

The two men were seated at the cluttered desk in room 603 of the Suffolk County Courthouse in Pemberton Square as the ever-present music played on a nearby radio. Although polite in outward appearance, there was an understated edge to the conversation. The two had known each other for several years, but they'd spent the last few working in the same building without ever speaking. Neither one chose to talk about why or how it happened, but there had been a palpable tension between the detective and the lawyer ever since the Frost trial.

Previously, if both men were waiting for a courthouse elevator, one would let the other board first and then wait for the next elevator to come along. Being in the same confined space meant the possibility of having to speak and resolve their differences. The next time they were both at the same elevator meant the first to board the last time had to wait.

And so it went, for years.

Two knuckleheads.

"This case means a lot to me," the detective began. "Her name is Holly Robins. It's the worst rape I ever saw, and I've seen a lot."

"OK," was the calculated and noncommittal response from the prosecutor on the opposite side of the metal desk.

"I've spent the last year and half of my life trying to figure it out and find the son of a bitch that did it."

It was clear Rose was driven, connected to the case in a way that transcended the norm of what was expected of any cop. There was no outward explanation for Rose's motivation to solve this crime. Perhaps it was the thought of protecting the women he loved. Maybe it was the just the thought of evening the score for someone who was a victim. Whatever the reason, Rose was there in room 603. He was a proud guy, so Burke knew the case had to be important to him to ask for help.

Burke knew about being obsessed with a case. He sensed the same consuming compulsion in Rose.

"I'd be glad to help you, Reggie," the lawyer said, extending his right hand. "Where do you want to start?"

THE SEARCHERS

The first movie Burke ever saw was a cowboy flick directed by John Ford. It starred "the Duke" and Natalie Wood.

The storyline went beyond the usual Western fare, telling the tale of an ex-Confederate soldier, Ethan Edwards, played by John Wayne, who returns to Texas after the Civil War. Shortly after his return, a band of renegade Comanche led by a chief named Scar massacres Edwards's family. Two of Edwards's nieces are kidnapped; the oldest is later raped and murdered, and the younger, Debbie, played by Natalie Wood, is held captive and later taken as Scar's wife.

For the next five years, Edwards and his brother's adopted son, Martin Pawley, relentlessly search the Western frontier, from Canada to Mexico, to find Ethan's niece, Debbie. The search becomes a compulsion, an obsession borne out of racism and hatred for Native Americans.

Burke was ten years old when he first saw *The Searchers*. It was one of his favorite movies.

Strange the way life imitates art.

Twenty-five years later, there were moments in each case when Burke saw himself in the role of one of the "searchers." In his mind, he was like the Duke, a loner on an uncertain search to find a missing person or the criminals responsible for a horrible crime. The motive wasn't the same, but the goal of simple justice was.

Burke wanted to ask the detective if he had ever seen the movie and if he knew who Martin Pawley was as they sat talking in room 603. He was certain Rose would feign ignorance and say something like, "Didn't he play for the Red Sox in the early sixties?"

The lawyer paused awkwardly and instead said nothing.

Rose seized the moment and continued by explaining the importance of Holly's case and what it meant to him to be a police officer. Burke hesitated before responding, realizing Rose had chosen to refer to himself as a "police officer" rather than use the word "cop."

The choice of words signified the respect Rose had for his job, an attitude driven by an inner need to protect those who weren't strong. Burke wanted to ask the detective about his past, what motivated him, how he got where he was, but Rose wasn't biting. In many ways, the police officer was like the lawyer, detached and brooding, constantly calculating and evaluating the stream of players interacting with his day-to-day existence. He never ever let anyone get too close.

"Why don't you tell me what you know about the case so far," the lawyer suggested as an open-ended introduction to the story of the Beacon Hill rapist.

It was just what was needed to open the dialogue. The pair talked for hours as Rose methodically went over the investigation. He described the false leads and the empty promise of hair and bloodstains found at the scene at Revere Street, but with no suspect for comparison. It was a tedious process. When he was done, the detective felt better for the first time in a long while.

"So after hearing all that, you got any ideas?" Rose asked.

"Yeah, I think there're probably a hundred guys out there that could have done this," Burke started slowly.

"Maybe more." The detective nodded.

"You said there was no evidence of a forced entry, so how was he able to get inside the apartment? It's on the fourth floor, right?"

"Yeah, it is. We're not sure how he got inside either. There's a security door on the ground floor, and the door to the victim's apartment was locked. We're sure of that."

"Is there a rear entrance?"

"Just a fire escape, but no real access to it."

"Did you run a check on any of the prerelease centers to see if there was anyone in the area that fit this pattern?"

"Yeah, there were a couple of possibilities," Rose said. "We found one guy who was late getting back to the halfway house for his curfew on the night of the rape, but there was nothing else to link him to the crime."

"So you've got no basis to get a search warrant for a sample of his hair or blood and compare it to the evidence you found at the crime scene?"

"No, nothing at all, it's just kind of a blank slate."

"Anybody else?" Burke asked.

"No, just the usual dirtbags, nobody that really fits this kind of violent profile."

"I think we need to get some publicity on this case. Whoever it was that raped Holly, you know it wasn't his first time. This guy knew exactly what to do, how to cover his tracks, the blindfold, the mouthwash, making sure he doesn't leave any fingerprints. This guy's a big-time 'skinner.' He took his time because he likes it. He's done this before. He hates women. He gets off on the power, the control. Chances are there's more than one victim out there with a similar fact pattern."

"Finding another one is a long shot at best," Rose said.

"I know, especially since it's been so long since the rape happened. I have a friend who might be willing to help us. She's got a lot of friends in the media. Publicity's the only way we're ever going to be able to resurrect Holly's case. You're not thinkin' of giving up, are you?" the lawyer asked.

"Nope. How 'bout you?"

"That'll be the day," Burke said to Rose, using his best John Wayne imitation.

VICTORIA BLOCK

Another former New Yorker who had made the transition north, she was bold and brassy, with fine-boned, almost angular high cheekbones and curly, red-tinged hair. She had the kind of raspy, readily identified voice that wasn't suited for the big screen. Victoria Block had long legs, a twin sister, and a penchant for asking the hard questions to a squirming public official on the take or a felony-prone mutt on the dodge from the law. She was one hell of a news reporter, working her way from the radio circuit to full-time television news.

The ninety-one days of spring that year were more rain and mud than sun. Like the weather, the Red Sox fielded another year of failed promise.

"Are you still talkin' to me?" the lawyer asked anxiously over the phone.

"You mean after you broke my fuckin' nose?"

"Racquetball is a tough sport. You were behind me. I couldn't see you. It was an accident. You left that drop shot out there and then came up from behind me when I swung. I didn't mean to hit you. I'm sorry, really."

"My parents think I should sue you. Now my sister says she's better looking than me. I don't know how much worse it could get. Did you just call to apologize again?"

There was a second when Burke thought better of asking Victoria for a favor. Maybe it was better to pull up stakes and move on. *Try someone else,* he thought and then knew at the same time that Reggie would be disappointed. It would be viewed as a failure.

"No, I called because I've got this rape case and the only way we're going to have any chance of solving it is to get it some airtime. The guy is a serial rapist, he likes what he does, and he's going to do it again if we don't

43

get him. Can you get this piece aired? It would mean a lot to one of the cops who's been working on the case for over a year now."

There was a lingering moment of hesitation as the reporter weighed her options.

"Of course I'll help," she told him.

WATER BABY

Each time she came into Burke's office, Ginnie Freeman tried to hide the now-whitened scars on her wrists with a long-sleeve blouse. Despite her muscular swimmer's shoulders, she appeared thin, not painfully, but enough to make her self-conscious at times.

A young woman from the South Shore of Boston who trusted too much, she was kidnapped at knifepoint near Faneuil Hall by two sadists from East Boston. They repeatedly raped and stabbed her in the backseat of her car and then tossed her naked and unconscious into Boston Harbor. They left her to drown in the murky water and then set her car on fire to destroy any evidence of their crime. The pair didn't know that Ginnie could swim since she was an infant and that the freezing cold water would revive her. She survived and swam to shore. Two days later she positively identified both men from over 750 arrest pictures taken by Boston police.

Ginnie still bore the scars on her arms and wrists from the cuts from their knife. She walked with the slightest trace of a limp from the four-inch blade that had been jammed into her thigh. Each step provided her with a never-ending reminder of the horror of that night, a savage souvenir from the beasts within the two men who had raped and tried to kill her.

The water baby's case was supposed to be Burke's last trial as a prosecutor. It was intended to be a final farewell to the ordered regiment of forensic pursuit amid the presence of arbitrary violence.

Burke had quietly promised himself, *When this trial is over, I'm going to put it all behind me. No more bad dreams, no more rapes or murders. No more music playing at 110 decibels to drown out the thoughts, the fear, and the memories.*

Sometimes things never seem to work out the way you plan.

"I've had three car accidents since that night," Ginnie told him in an attempt to make sense of the crime, their crime, and now in a twisted way it had somehow become her crime too.

Burke knew better than to interrupt. The scars on Ginnie's body paled in comparison to those hidden within her mind.

"I can't concentrate. I don't remember things like I used to. There's just this feeling. Like I'm unsure, I doubt and question myself about everything. Who am I? Why did I let them into my car? I should have known better. It's become an issue of trust now. I look at everyone differently since that day, and somehow I think everyone looks at me differently now, too."

He understood her uncertainty. Burke looked at everybody differently too. He didn't say it, but there had been an unexplained loss of trust and innocence for him too.

Ginnie hesitated before she spoke again.

"Then I think about why I survived, being able to swim ever since I was a baby. Like maybe it was God's plan all along. Like He gave me the ability, the strength to overcome what was done to me," the young woman said, somehow still searching for an answer.

"Yeah, maybe He did," Burke agreed.

"I'm just so afraid that I'm going to forget something at trial and get all screwed up. I don't want to disappoint you," Ginnie said with a simple vulnerability.

"You won't. Don't worry, I'll get us through this," Burke told her, and then just as quickly he regretted saying it.

The trial of the two sadists from East Boston started the following morning.

It was a nondescript day, no extreme of weather or news item to separate it from any other. What was unique was the first meeting of the young woman and the two men since the night of the ride from hell.

"I don't think I can do this," Ginnie told Burke in a last-minute moment of doubt outside the double wooden doors leading into the courtroom.

"Yes, you can," he reassured her as the two entered the drab room together and walked slowly toward the witness stand.

David Giacalone was the lesser of the two defendants. His partner, Michael Quarto, was an ugly open sore, a sawed-off, sadistic piece of human garbage who had taken particular pleasure in twisting the knife back and forth in the leg of the young woman begging for mercy in the backseat of her car.

The water baby took the stand and sat calmly in the straight-backed witness chair facing the two men who had raped, beaten, and left her for dead. She raised her eyes to look up and then, in a quiet moment, realized for the first time that she had survived for a reason. The two men somehow seemed smaller, less threatening to her as the morning sun poured through the austere courtroom windows on the eighth floor of the courthouse. She felt a rush of strength as she began to speak.

"My name is Ginnie Freeman," she said softly, introducing herself to the jury.

The jurors craned their necks as they listened in shock and horror to her story.

"I ask you to look around the courtroom and tell me if you see the two men who raped you that night?" Burke asked his witness at the conclusion of her testimony.

"Yes, I do," Ginnie responded calmly as she pointed to the defendants' table. "They're both seated right over there."

THE BROOKE HOUSE

It had the kind of name one would associate with a politically connected social club or a snooty, high-end private school, but it was far from either. The Brooke House was a prerelease center anonymously located at 79 Chandler Street in the South End of Boston.

Intended for offenders making the transition from a correctional institution into full release, the five-story brick building housed up to fifty short-timers in a casual dormitory setting. A Cinderella curfew at midnight required the inmates to return to the prerelease center on time or risk return to the higher-security institutions they had originated from.

Many inmates used the opportunity of prerelease to make an earnest reentry into society. Others took advantage of the minimum-security setting and employed it as a springboard for more violent crimes, concealed by the public perception of a more structured environment.

Louis Pina was one of the latter. A serial rapist from Norwich, Connecticut, Pina was forty years old and currently serving the downside of an unrelated five-to-seven-year sentence for the rape of a woman beaten into submission three years earlier. The prerelease center at the Brooke House gave him hours of unsupervised time alone on the street, enough to become familiar with the Boston area, including Beacon Hill.

In 1978, Pina scaled the fire escape of the four-story, brick apartment building located in the rear of 49 Revere Street. Once inside the apartment, he raped a nineteen-year-old Boston University psychology student. He was never identified or charged with that crime. Pina met his victim days later on Boston Common and apologized to her for his "animalistic" behavior. For whatever reason, the nineteen-year-old forgave him and chose not to prosecute her attacker. Pina was free to rape again.

49

Five years later, in 1983, while a resident at the Brooke House serving out his sentence for a third rape, Pina returned to 49 Revere Street, climbed the same rusty fire escape, and raped Holly Robins.

Although Holly had been Pina's most recent victim, he had been able to escape detection by blindfolding her for all but a brief moment before the attack began.

"Hey, Detective Rose, you've got a call on line seventeen. It's about the Beacon Hill rape case," the cadet announced loudly as he pointed feverishly with his right hand to the receiver held in his left.

The walls of the detective's office on the fourth floor of Area A were a mishmash of mementos and photographs of Rose's family. A life chronicle of his past spent on a remote dock in the woods of Maine or at the kids' birthdays in his backyard or the kitchen of his house in Medford. The images grounded and motivated him. He glanced up at the picture of his wife with her smile as he simultaneously grasped the phone from the cradle.

"This is Detective Reggie Rose."

"I heard the news reports about that man, the man that broke into the apartment on Revere Street," the unidentified woman began haltingly.

"OK," Rose answered quietly.

"I used to live there."

Cops get phone calls every day, dozens of them, but Rose knew the significance of this call when the soft female voice said the words "I used to live there."

The detective could feel his pulse quicken and the fine dark hairs on the back of his neck begin to rise. He clenched the phone tightly in his fist, praying that the caller wouldn't hang up before he could get her name; there was no way to trace her call. A simultaneous feeling of hopelessness and exhilaration raced through his body. His mind went temporarily blank as he sought out the perfect words with which to respond.

"I need to talk to you, please," Rose said, easing out a strained plea.

"I'm not going to testify against him, but I know his name. He raped me too, in the same apartment. There on Revere Street," the stranger's voice explained, holding the possible answer to the mystery of Holly's case in the temporary fleeting connection between them.

"All I need for now is his name. This guy won't stop unless we catch him. You know he'll hurt other women. I know you don't want that to

50

happen. That's why you're calling me. You don't want this to happen to anyone else, do you?" Rose explained softly as the suddenness and the shock of the call made him begin to sweat and his heart race.

"No, I don't, but I'm so ashamed. I just can't…"

The detective sensed the young woman would end the call, that he would lose the one chance he was ever likely to have to identify Holly's attacker. He could hear the words rush out of his mouth as he tried to make an emotional connection.

"We can get you some help. You don't need to spend the rest of your life feeling like this."

"Am I going to have to testify?"

"That's not up to me, but let me tell you about the other woman this guy raped. She's kind. You'd like her. She was young, probably just like you. She wasn't experienced at sex, and when she wouldn't submit, he beat her. He beat her bad. And just like you she felt so ashamed, like somehow it was her fault. But you and I both know it wasn't her fault, was it?"

"No, it wasn't her fault." The caller paused. "It was mine."

It wasn't the response the detective expected.

There was an extended moment of quiet as Rose sensed the young woman was struggling with the decision whether to release the raging demon from within her mind.

The answer came sooner than he thought.

"His name is Pina. Louis Pina," she told the detective as he broke the lead in the yellow pencil, struggling to scribble as quickly as he could on the yellow legal pad.

CHRIS CASNER

After the anonymous telephone conversation, Rose got a listing of all the former tenants for the fourth-floor apartment at 49 Revere Street and began the process of elimination. It didn't take long to find out who the caller was who identified Louis Pina as her assailant. It was the Boston University student who had been raped by Pina in 1978. There was an aura of tragedy about the young woman as she repeatedly refused to cooperate or testify against the man who had attacked her.

"I told you who he was, and that's all I'm going to do. I'm not going back there again," she told the detective, ending the conversation.

Rose didn't stop. He got the names and current addresses for the reluctant victim's roommates and set up an appointment.

The BU student's roommate's name was Chris Casner. She was tall and lean, imbued with a Brooks Brothers style, accented by a silk ascot hanging neatly between the stays of her starched pinpoint collar. She readily fielded the detective's questions nearly seven years after the first rape at 49 Revere Street.

A twenty-five-year-old paralegal working in a prestigious downtown law firm, Casner was accustomed to the demands of both lawyers and clients. The interview with Reggie Rose was a piece of cake, vanilla, but with a thin veneer of bitter lemon frosting.

"I heard about the other girl on the news, the one that was just raped. Once I heard it, I had this creepy feeling 'cause my old roommate and my sister and I all lived in the same apartment on Revere Street, ya know? When that reporter gave the description of the guy, I knew it was him. Something inside me told me it was Pina. I feel so bad for this poor other girl, Holly," Chris explained while Rose simultaneously nodded and took notes.

Casner was a wealth of information.

"I know how Pina got inside the kitchen windows too. I've seen my boyfriend do it a couple of times when I locked myself out of the apartment. You can swing over from the top of the fire escape and get in that way. We never used to lock the kitchen window."

"You know your former roommate won't testify against him now, don't you? We've had her held as a material witness, and she still refuses to help us," the detective explained.

"Yes, she called me and told me that. I'm so sorry. The thing is, I remember Pina sitting at the table eating dinner in our apartment. Can you believe it? This is the same guy that broke in here and raped my roommate. She thought she could help him. That's why she invited him back there, to counsel him. Oh my God. I mean I love her. I grew up with her and she was my friend, but the only reason he didn't hurt her like he did Holly was because she didn't resist. She didn't fight back. I wanted to scream every time I saw him."

"Are you kidding?" Rose exclaimed as his head shook slowly from side to side. "Do you think you could identify this guy if we showed you some photographs?"

"I know I could," the young woman declared with certainty.

"There's something else I need to ask you," Rose began. "Are you willing to testify? This isn't going to be an easy case, especially since your roommate won't testify. You'll become the focus of the defense attorney's cross-examination. They can try to bring up stuff about your past that you may not want to come out."

There was a brief pause while the young woman weighed her options. She thought of her friend and then about Pina's second victim, shuddering at the horror both had endured.

"Yes, I want to testify. I *need* to testify. I need to help Holly. What's more important, I need to do this for me, too."

There was a momentary hesitation as the detective waited for the other shoe to drop.

"I'm tired of feeling like damaged goods. I was raped when I was just a kid. I was afraid and did nothing about it. I'm not afraid anymore. I'm going to help you."

INDICTMENT

An indictment is a formal charge initiated through the vote of twenty-three grand jurors who hear evidence and decide if there is probable cause to believe that a defendant has committed the crime.

"I went back behind the apartment building on 49 Revere Street just to see if the son of a bitch could have climbed the fire escape," Rose told the lawyer as they spoke over the phone a week after the meeting with Chris Casner.

"And...?"

"It's not easy, but he could have done it."

"How do you know that?"

"Because I did it too. I jumped up to the bottom rung and pulled myself up. He's younger than I am," Rose said with a small twisted smile of satisfaction.

Burke wanted to say, "Good job," but he felt the detective wouldn't have seen climbing the fire escape as anything other than his responsibility, an obligatory duty to a victim, nothing more. It was all part of building a case. Besides, neither one of them was into hearts and flowers.

The lawyer sent the conversation in another direction.

"You know the fact Pina was in that apartment before could hurt us, especially since his first victim won't testify. Pina can claim he consensually had sex with the first woman and that's why we found his pubic hair there and matched it with hairs we found after Holly's rape. It's a perfectly logical explanation."

There was a gagging feeling rising in his throat as Rose realized proving Pina was in the apartment five years ago could help the defense.

"Yeah, that could hurt us in front of a jury, couldn't it?"

"It could, Reggie, it could. Then it becomes easy for a jury to think there's a reasonable doubt in the case. But I still think we need to put him there to show his familiarity with the place. We also need someone to testify that you can get into the apartment from the fire escape through the kitchen window."

"Right, there's nothing below you four floors down once you're at the top of the fire escape. You've got to be strong enough to swing yourself over to the kitchen windows to get in the apartment."

"We've got another problem too with the timing of the rape and Pina's possible alibi that he was back at the prerelease center," Burke said.

"What is it?"

"I spoke to the people at the Brooke House about their records on the night of the rape. We know that the curfew was midnight and Pina was late that night. He made it back at just about twelve forty-five in the morning. The rape takes place between ten thirty p.m. and twelve thirty a.m. So not only do we have to prove Pina was at the apartment that night, we also have to be able to show he could have made it back to Chandler Street from Revere Street in less than fifteen minutes."

"That's cutting it close. You're the runner. Think you can make it from Revere to Chandler that quick?" Rose challenged the lawyer.

"Yeah, I think I could, but I wouldn't be able to testify about it if I did and still prosecute the case. Looks like you're going to have to do it. Or do you want me to find someone else a little younger out of the academy to give it a shot?" Burke asked with a straight face.

"Yeah, that'll be the day," John Wayne's imitator responded with his best cowboy drawl.

The following morning, Rose made the run from 49 Revere Street to the Brooke House in his best Nikes in just over twelve minutes, running past Mount Vernon to Beacon Street, across the Boston Common to Columbus Avenue and onto Chandler. When he was done, he went back and made the trip a second time. He knocked fifteen-seconds off his first attempt. The distance was just over a mile and a half.

"How come you're so out of breath?" Burke asked when he received the call from Rose. "You just finish the run from Beacon Hill?"

"No, but I got some good news for you. I was talking to the supervisor at the Brooke House about Pina. He reminded me that the bastard left his wallet when he got shipped out and sent back to Concord prison. They gave it to me back then, and the wallet's been sitting here in my office at Area A in a manila envelope ever since."

56

"OK and…?"

"I just went through it, and guess what I found inside his wallet?"

"I dunno," the lawyer said blankly, anticipating Pina's claim of privacy rights in his abandoned property.

"You're not going to believe this. I found two tickets to—"

"*Amadeus*," the lawyer interrupted, completing the sentence for him.

"Yup."

"Holy shit, Reggie," Burke kept repeating to the detective.

*****

Rose had made hundreds of appearances at the grand jury room on the seventh floor of the courthouse. None meant more to him than Holly's case. The testimony before the panel of twenty-three citizens was crisp, professional, and without elaboration. Probable cause was the goal, not proof beyond a reasonable doubt. The members of the panel had heard every kind of case over the course of their preceding months of service. The process became numbing over time, with some jurors nodding into a semiconscious state of monotony during their eight-hour day listening about crime and detection.

The case of the Beacon Hill rapist was an early morning jolt to the grand jurors' senses. The group didn't need much more than the pictures of Holly's face, coupled with the written statement from the first victim, the pubic hair samples found at the scene, and the *Amadeus* tickets discovered in Pina's wallet to make up their minds.

Burke directed the inquiry of Rose in a straightforward series of questions and answers. The investigation that had taken over two years to complete required only twenty minutes to get indictments for the charges of aggravated rape and breaking and entering a dwelling with the intent to commit a felony.

The trial wouldn't be as quick or as easy.

When the indictments were returned by the grand jury, Burke wanted to tell Rose that he was leaving the DA's office, that he wouldn't be the one to try Holly's case, but he knew he would be seen as a failure in the detective's eyes. There was no gray area for Reggie. You either succeeded or you failed. It wouldn't matter what had been done up to that point.

THE ROOM OF DOOM

Ancient in appearance, with ten rows of long, heavy wooden benches, the courtroom referred to as the "First Session" seemed like it had been in place since before the turn of the century. It was the "Room of Doom" for many of those who just happened to be passing through as a criminal defendant. Justice got dispensed there, in large and small doses, depending on your viewpoint, and which side of the case you were situated on.

Constructed in 1937, and precariously situated nearly halfway between the fifteen stories of the courthouse in Pemberton Square, the "First" was the epicenter of every serious criminal case in America's greatest city. It was the largest courtroom in the building. All the arraignments, preliminary motion hearings, trial assignments, and offers to plead guilty were held there each day.

There was a comfortable air of familiarity for Burke as he effortlessly passed through the double swinging doors of the First Session that warm day in mid-February. The opening of spring training camp for the Sox was a week away, and most of the pitchers and catchers had already reported.

The prosecutor had been in the courtroom hundreds of times before and knew most of the clerks, stenographers, probation officers, court officers, and attorneys present on a first-name basis.

The Room of Doom was the gathering point for those lawyers engaged in the unique world of "foxes and hounds." Although it was a major city, the criminal defense bar in Boston consisted of a relatively small group of attorneys. The names of the defendants changed daily, but as a prosecutor you dealt with the same circle of defense lawyers on a regular basis. Both sides knew most of the opposition either by name or reputation. Many current defense attorneys had earned their spurs as former prosecutors.

Burke briefly thought about the same career transition as he quickly strode toward the microphone placed at the podium facing the silver-haired judge. There was an unexpected sense of loss as he realized Louis Pina might be his final case as a prosecutor.

It was the first time he had seen Pina in person. The defendant sat alone, with his head bowed, his eyes on the floor and his face angled away from the public glare of the television camera on the opposite side of the courtroom. He was forty-one years old and knew what to expect. Pina had been through an arraignment for rape before. He wore a silver-gray barracuda jacket with the narrow collar pulled unconvincingly up around each side of his jawline to hide from the unblinking lens of the camera.

There was a moment of pause as Burke waited for the presiding judge to give him the "I'm ready to listen" signal. When it finally came, the buzz from the courtroom had ebbed to a quiet blanket of anticipation.

"The victim was a young woman, twenty-two years old, who was alone in her bedroom that night," the prosecutor recited calmly to the judge as if he was reading from a prepared text.

The summary was a clinical presentation of the facts, designed to provide enough information to ensure the defendant would be held without bail, but not enough substance to give the entire case away to the defense.

"It was approximately ten thirty in the evening when the victim heard a noise coming from the windows in her kitchen. Entry was gained through an unlocked kitchen window. She was subsequently blindfolded. A blouse was placed over her face. She attempted to fight her attacker off. She could only describe him as a black man with a mustache and of medium build," the prosecutor explained, building to a gruesome crescendo.

Burke paused long enough to turn his head and look at Pina before continuing.

"The defendant repeatedly raped the victim more than ten times vaginally, orally, and anally over a period of the next two and a half hours. He beat her unmercifully."

Pina never raised his head, content to wait out the words that confronted him with the reality of his deeds. It was all like a dream to the defendant seated on the wooden bench. He heard the white man in the white shirt and the gray suit talking about somebody else, a stranger, in a time and place somehow detached, disconnected from the person he knew himself to be.

"The victim was beaten about the face. There was a tremendous amount of blood throughout the apartment," Burke explained as he handed a color photograph of an unrecognizable Holly Robins to the clerk. The clerk blanched and averted his eyes after glancing at the likeness, and then he handed it over to the stoic judge, who in turn passed it quickly back.

His Honor didn't say it, but you could sense he was wondering how the blindfolded victim could possibly make any identification of the man who raped her. Pina would be released on bail and be back on the streets unless there was a further explanation from the Commonwealth. There was no choice but to reveal the facts about Pina's first victim five years earlier.

He hadn't initially intended to, but Burke explained this wasn't the first time Louis Pina had assaulted someone inside the apartment at 49 Revere Street. At the end of the monologue, he asked that Pina be held without bail pending trial.

Outside the First Session, the three female reporters from the Boston-area television stations wanted to know more about the strange coincidence of Pina's two victims.

By the time of the evening news, the news stations had more information about Pina. The anchor for Channel 7 began the piece by echoing the prosecutor's statements, telling the ready audience this wasn't the first time Pina had been to Revere Street.

"Another woman the man allegedly raped seven years ago finally breaks her silence about that attack. Now police say that both these attacks took place in the same Beacon Hill apartment. New England news reporter Rehema Ellis is here now with what investigators are calling a very strange case. Rehema..."

Striking in appearance and attire, Rehema Ellis was one of the first black female reporters to crack the racial barrier in a racially divided city. She had been seated in the courtroom during the arraignment that day, silently taking notes amid the crowd of regulars.

As she began to speak, the camera cut to the scene of the crime.

"The attack occurred here on Revere Street in a top-floor apartment," the reporter announced, gesturing back over her right shoulder toward the red front door at number 49.

As she spoke the camera panned upward to the top floor of the brick building.

"Police say Louis Pina had been here at least once before, five years earlier. That's when another woman was raped in the very same apartment, but she kept silent about her attacker until hearing of the 1983 case and thinking that the same man committed the rape. The man named was Louis Pina. The DA's office says that authorities have matched the suspect's hair and blood samples with evidence found at the crime scene. Authorities also said that help from the first victim was critical in identifying a suspect. When asked why she didn't come forward sooner, counselors at a rape crisis center said she was probably just too afraid."

Channel 5 had a similar explanation to their viewers that evening as Natalie Jacobson introduced Krista Bradford, the spot reporter broadcasting first from the crime scene and then from nearby Boston Common.

"It was brutal," Bradford began. "They said there was so much blood in the apartment on Revere Street it looked as if a murder had been committed there. Instead, it was the savage beating and rape of a twenty-two-year-old," the earnest reporter explained.

"Pina became the prime suspect in the case after a former psychology major identified him—a woman who claimed she was raped in the same house, in the same way, by the same man five years before." As Bradford spoke, the camera panned in sync, closer and closer to the red front door at 49 Revere Street.

"A man who, in both cases, apologized to his victims," the reporter followed with a note of incredulity.

"The first crime victim didn't report the crime sooner because she allegedly felt sorry for the very person who raped her. The suspect reportedly approached her right here on Boston Common and begged for her forgiveness. She not only forgave him, but she gave him informal counseling sessions for over a month. The therapy didn't work. Pina was transferred to the Brooke House after serving nearly four years in prison for his second alleged rape. He was transferred here to the halfway house for good behavior, but this new home gave him the opportunity to commit rape for a third time. If convicted, he could be sentenced to life," the reporter closed as the news shot shifted from Boston Common to a clip of the Brooke House.

At the end of each story, the anchors reassured their anxious viewers that the Beacon Hill rapist had been held at Charles Street Jail without bail.

HOLLY

In many ways Holly Robins was like Ginnie Freeman, the "water baby." Holly was another unsuspecting innocent caught in an evil web of arbitrary and indiscriminate violence.

It was to be the last of many meetings between the prosecutor and the victim in his cramped office at the courthouse. There was a sense of trust between them, melded from the numerous occasions spent discussing the trial process, the evidence in Holly's case, and the uncertainty of a conviction. The lawyer was reluctant to be hopeful, fearing the ever-present possibility of an acquittal. He tempered Holly's expectations with stories of other cases and the unpredictability of a jury's reasoning. Through it all, Holly remained buoyant, a survivor.

"I don't know if I ever told you, but my grandfather died the day after I was raped. We were so close. He came to Boston to be with my dad and me, to help me. He saw my face. It was so bad, so swollen and bruised. I should never have let him see me that way. My grandfather was so sad. He couldn't talk. He just sat in a chair and cried. The next day, he had a heart attack and died."

Holly's voice drifted into a soft flow of gasps and tears, searching for a measure of understanding in an uncaring world. Much of Burke's job was spent listening to victims. Innocent people previously untouched by the specter of violence, which for reasons unknown had chosen them. Individuals selected as a life experiment in brutality, then left broken, struggling to make sense out of the cards they had been dealt. A hopeless hand with no winners, cast away with only the sense of an unexplained, unrelenting loss.

"It's almost like my grandfather was a victim too. You know what I mean? I think he just felt so helpless."

"Yes, I think I know what you mean," the prosecutor told her without explanation.

There was an awkward pause as the young woman gathered the words in her mind before she spoke.

"I talked to Reggie Rose. He told me you were going to leave the DA's office. Is that true?"

"Yes, Holly. It is. I'm sorry, but there are many other really good assistants here who can take over your case," Burke said in a monotone without an expression of enthusiasm.

"But Timmy, you can't just walk away. I don't know any of those other assistants like I know you. This just isn't fair. Please don't do this to me, to my family," Holly pleaded as the flow of tears trickled down her cheeks.

Life gives you moments. Moments when you make decisions that define who you are and how you live your life. Choices about the things you do to help or ignore those who need you. The opportunities that God gives you the ability, the gift to make a difference, if you choose to.

Burke was given that choice, that opportunity. The option to do what was right for Holly Robins, but he was too cold, too distant from the heart-beat of life, left uncaring by the life he had seen, felt, and lived. He bit the inside of his left cheek in a vain attempt to feel pain, to feel something.

"No, Holly, I'm sorry. I can't," Burke told her without more explanation.

THE STEAMING KETTLE

"We'll always have your office available if you ever decide to come back to the district attorney's office," the first assistant offered the younger lawyer as they sat talking over a bowl of thick clam chowder in the Steaming Kettle restaurant.

Overhead, "Everybody's Talkin' At Me" meshed with the everyday chatter of the patrons.

A palpable mist hung in the air outside the crowded space as the two men hunched over their bowls. Located across busy Tremont Street, a four-minute walk from the courthouse, the corner café was the mixing pot for defendants, witnesses, judges, and clerks, as well as prosecution and defense lawyers alike. Above the entrance, the large polished copper-colored kettle percolated a small cloud of finely boiled steam into the heavier gray haze.

"Thanks, Paul, but it's time to move on," Burke told his mentor, calling Mr. Leary by his first name for the first time.

He knew there was no turning back from his decision to leave the DA's office. While that much was clear, there were other doubts that haunted his mind. Surrounded by the recurring presence of murder and rape, death and violence in its worst forms, he had forgotten the meaning of life and lost his ability to love. Burke couldn't openly express the thought to himself or to anyone else for that matter, but he had begun to question his belief in God. Like some of the victims in his cases, he had grown cold and dead to the world around him.

Burke steeled his mind not to care, hiding his emotions from those closest to him. No one got inside. No one even scratched the surface. He found himself searching for an answer that never came, his thoughts a quiet storm. Music became a refuge, with each drive to and from work

67

accompanied by a mind-numbing incessant beat played at 110 decibels. The dark rhythm of Santana's "Oye Como Va" was the music of choice, propelling him into a glazed state of perpetual numbness.

It was a slow, insidious process that had occurred over the past several years, a gradual and dehumanizing erosion of a belief in humanity. With each conviction came a new case, another horror story of human carnage to be studied, investigated, and prosecuted. His résumé had become a bloody wasteland of cadavers and misery.

"You never really told us the reason you were leaving when the district attorney got your letter of resignation," the older man said as he raised his eyebrows and tilted his head toward his companion.

A pregnant pause filled the dead air.

"Everything OK at home?" Leary probed.

"Yeah, everything's fine," Burke fudged, afraid to show any emotion.

He wanted to tell Mr. Leary of his loss of faith, that he prayed to a God he didn't believe in, but there was no way to explain his life or what he had lost.

"So why do you want to leave?"

"It's just kind of a personal decision. You know that I love what I do here, but it's just time for me to make a change in my life. Sometimes things happen to you that change you, and then it's *you* that needs to make a change," the lawyer offered vaguely, unwilling and unable to place the words to his thoughts.

Leary nodded in apparent acquiescence.

"Listen, I know we threw you into the snake pit at an early age. You've seen a lot of death since you've been here, some really, really, bad stuff, things that I know you weren't used to. The murder of the mother and two kids was horrible, the worst that life has to offer, but jeepers creepers, you've made one heck of a difference to so many people. Hell, you even put a serial killer away for the rest of his life. I don't know many lawyers that can say that."

Burke smiled politely at his mentor's use of the phrase "jeepers creepers" as he momentarily thought of Lenny "the Quahog" Paradiso's conviction.

"I appreciate you saying that, but I'm looking forward to going into private practice and trying something new. It'll be different, that's for sure. Another guy from our office is going to join me," Burke explained.

"Who's that?"

"It's Mark Newman. We just signed a lease to rent some office space in Faneuil Hall."

"Well, I was hoping you might change your mind about going into private practice and decide to stay here. Maybe I should have shared this with you sooner, but now that you decided to leave, I think there's something you should know about yourself."

"OK, what is it?" the lawyer asked without truly wanting to know what the answer was.

"It's just that you can't change who you are. It's not going to be any different for you on the outside. You're drawn to these kinds of cases, and somehow they always seem to find you too," Leary told him quietly.

Burke nodded in agreement, without fully knowing why.

"There's one last thing," Leary added without waiting for a response. "The district attorney has asked me to impose on you to try the Louis Pina case."

"I'd like to, Paul, but Pina's trial isn't scheduled for another nine months. If I don't leave now, I'll never leave."

"That won't be a problem. You can go out on your own, and we can have you appointed as a special prosecutor for this one trial. You'd be able to go into private practice and still try this one remaining case. I know Reggie Rose and the victim's family would appreciate it, too. It's just not like you to leave something unfinished like this."

In his mind, Burke saw Holly's face and remembered her plea. He knew he had been given an opportunity to help her and callously chose to reject it. Second chances to correct your mistakes didn't come along that often.

There was a momentary hesitation as he weighed his options and turned to face his mentor.

"All right, Paul, I'll do it, but this has to be my last case, OK?"

"Thank you, Timmy. I knew you'd do the right thing." Leary smiled, already certain what the other lawyer's decision would be.

The two men stood, walked toward the door, briefly shook hands beneath the polished copper dome, and then headed in very different directions.

5 FANEUIL HALL

Despite the desire to make a change, Burke felt empty for days after he left the DA's office. He had always been a loner by choice, but now without the familiar trappings of the courthouse, there was an even greater sense of isolation.

His new office at 5 Faneuil Hall was perched on the fourth floor of the North Market building in the heart of Boston. Built before the American Revolution, the North Market was a brick four-story former warehouse recently converted to office and retail space in historic Faneuil Hall.

Faneuil Hall Marketplace is four separate structures: the North and South Markets, Quincy Market, and the original Faneuil Hall building built in 1742. The urban center to a renovated Boston, the location attracted millions of visitors each year in the eighties, even more than Disneyland. With dozens of push carts, shops, food stalls, nearly twenty restaurants, bars, street clowns, mimes, and jugglers, it was a destination for visitors from around the world.

Burke would now call it home.

His office space was a well-laid-out expanse of exposed brick and wooden beams, with each wall adorned by framed prints ranging from Claude Monet to Andrew Wyeth and Winslow Homer. Large stretches of window glass provided a pigeon-eyed view of the thousands of tourists passing beneath each day. *Bustling* was probably the word best suited to describe the flow of life and commerce wending its way between the rows of food choices in the domed center pavilion of Quincy Market.

Along with the three-year lease and the rent payments of four large each month came two shiny brass keys to the heavy oak and glass front door and the sense of starting over. It was September of 1985, and a brave new world waited.

The Olde Towne Team with Jim Rice, Billy Buck, Wade Boggs, and Marty Barrett was on its way to a fifth-place finish in a middling season of eighty-one wins and matching eighty-one losses; the Red Sox were a year away from the magic and heartbreak of the seventh game of the World Series against the New York Mets.

As a fledgling lawyer in private practice, Burke never knew with certainty what his source of clients would be. Referrals from friends, family, and past life connections offered a modest potential for new clients, but he could never be sure who would walk through his door in need of representation. The experience of being a prosecutor was a narrow field of expertise, offering little exposure to the civil side of the law. Many former DA's did the 180-degree flip, using their background in criminal law as a springboard to defending those accused of crimes, never venturing into the civil arena.

The former prosecutor didn't hesitate to make the jump to the civil side. He bought a copy of the Massachusetts Rules of Civil Procedure, read it from cover to cover, and invested more money than he had in a thirty-volume set of Massachusetts Practice Series, the how-to-do-it explanation for new practitioners.

The Material Girl was singing about a material world when the large guy in jeans and a ponytail announced his presence at the front door.

It was trooper Andrew Palombo.

Palombo was one of Burke's best friends. It was never "Andy." He always called him "Drew."

There was a comfortable relationship between the two men born out of a shared history that had evolved around the murder investigation and trial of Lenny "the Quahog" Paradiso two years earlier.

"Sweet digs," Drew remarked as he surveyed the scene. "You've come a long way from your little office at the courthouse. I see you still got your radio playing all the time."

"The music is cheap entertainment. All I need now is some clients to help pay the rent," the lawyer added as he smiled and rubbed his thumb over the pointer finger of his right hand.

"Well, I don't have any cases for you, but I do have some news. You remember the woman in the courtroom at the end of Paradiso's trial?"

"Yeah, you mean the one dressed in white?"

"Right, about a week ago I got a call from a woman who said Paradiso raped her back in the early seventies. She told me she didn't testify against him then back then, but she came to his trial on the day of the verdict to see what happened to him."

"Ya' think it was Florence White?"

"I don't know for sure. She wouldn't tell me her name. I asked her why she wouldn't testify against Lenny, and all she would say is that she was too ashamed," Drew explained, slowly shaking his large head from side to side.

"She sounds just like one of Louis Pina's first victims. She won't testify against him either. Says she's too embarrassed by what the defense can use against her on cross-examination."

"What are you going to do about it?" Drew asked.

"I had her recognized by the court as a material witness. So she has to attend the trial, but it's too risky for me to put her on the stand if she's not a willing participant. At the same time, if it weren't for her, we would never have found out who raped Holly Robins. So I feel obligated not to force her to testify, but even if I don't call her, the defense could. She's potentially radioactive for both of us," Burke said.

"Pina's trial is coming up soon, isn't it? How'd you feel about being back in court as a DA?"

"I'm not exactly sure, Drew," the former prosecutor said as he searched the space outside his new office window for an answer.

COURTROOM 808

The trial of Louis Pina was held in the same courtroom where Lenny Paradiso had been convicted of the murder of Marie Iannuzzi nearly two years earlier.

Time had passed, but things hadn't changed in courtroom 808.

The space was a minimal setting, with four rows of heavy, uncomfortable wooden benches and two unwieldy air conditioners that flanked both sides of the jury enclosure. When their switch was tripped, they whirled and wheezed incessantly, drowning out the testimony emanating from the nearby witness stand. Most summer days they were turned on only during recess, causing the jurors to resort to using their hands as auxiliary fans in the afternoon hours of testimony.

Hot in the summer and drafty cold in the winter, the large room had twenty-five-foot-high ceilings with sheets of peeling paint and wainscoted walls of an unknown type of wood that hadn't seen a scrub brush or a coat of shellac in decades. A built-in bookcase pinned behind the judge's bench held row upon row of appellate court decisions with brown bindings that were seldom used and never dusted. Next to it, a worn and faded Stars and Stripes stood a silent guard over each day's proceedings.

Remnants of the early morning sun poured in unfiltered through a large vertical window behind the witness stand, creating a backdrop of light that made it difficult to see the witness's eyes during direct or cross-examination. Adjoining the witness enclosure was an elevated but unremarkable wooden bench, where a stainless steel water pitcher and nondescript glass sat askew to the left of the judge's leather swivel chair; the lawyers had to drink from the fountain out in the hallway.

The former prosecutor still loved the old courtroom.

Despite its failures, justice got dispensed there, in large and small doses, depending of course on your point of view and which side of the case you happened to be situated on. Burke felt at ease as he passed through the enclosure that separated the attorneys' tables from the visitors' gallery.

Counsel for the defense was a pleasant, affable, and capable attorney appointed by the court to represent the defendant, after a disgruntled Pina complained that his first lawyer was white. Pina's newest attorney, John Laymon, was African American, a public defender, and accustomed to dealing with difficult clients and cases.

Bespectacled and soft-spoken, with just the hint of a Southern drawl, John Laymon was a formidable opponent with whom minority jurors readily identified. No piece of evidence went uncontested, no prosecution theory went unchallenged, and each Commonwealth witness would undergo a thorough cross-examination designed either to create contradiction or raise questions of credibility. In a city with a long history of racial tension, police witnesses were automatically suspect in the minds of many jurors, particularly in the case of the rape of a white woman by a black man.

The volatile issues of race and rape in criminal cases required an individualized voir dire, or questioning, of each potential juror by the presiding judge. He was a dour but able jurist with two first names. John Paul Sullivan was Irish-Catholic, Harvard-educated, and insisted on reference to both names. It wasn't John, Jon, or Johnny—the name was John Paul.

Burke took his place at the counsel table and set the large manila case file on the burnished oak table. He turned back to shake hands with Laymon and ignored the glare from Pina. He then looked to his right, expecting his friend Drew to be seated in his usual place. A smaller version from the Boston police had taken his spot.

The familiar "All rise" from one of the white-shirted court officers signaled the entrance of John Paul, as the parties and the assembled jurors in the gallery stood in unison, listening to the bark of "Hear ye, hear ye," and "God save the Commonwealth of Massachusetts" from a flushed, large-framed bailiff. There was a palpable tension, an unseen anxious energy about the old courtroom as the prospective jurors settled back into their collective seats on the hard wooden benches.

The trial was about to begin.

The cry from the court officer was closely followed by the judge's opening remarks to the jury, the introduction of the parties, and a brief inquiry to determine if any of the prospective jurors knew anyone on the inside of the lawyers' bar, anything about the case, or had formed any opinion about the guilt or innocence of the accused.

None did, or at least no one admitted to it.

The lawyers had heard the same questions dozens of times before. Instead of listening, they busily spent their time examining the questionnaires recently completed by the jurors regarding their ages, marital status, children, occupation, prior jury duty, and exposure to the legal system. The single sheet of paper, and a brief glimpse into each juror's potential bias while questioned by the judge, was all each lawyer had to determine whether they would accept or challenge a candidate for the jury box. Neither the race nor the gender of a juror could be used as a factor to disqualify their possible service. If you were the prosecutor, you'd better have a convincing reason for challenging a black juror.

As each potential juror was called up to the witness stand, they were asked the same series of questions about their personal biases and attitudes surrounding rape cases, racial animosity, the presumption of innocence, plus their ability and willingness to sit on a case of this significance. At the end of the day, nearly forty jurors had been interviewed, and only four made the cut. It was a long process. It would take another day to make an even dozen with two alternates.

Once the jury was empanelled and sworn in, each attorney would have the opportunity to address the panel about their respective theories of the case. John Paul wasn't happy about Burke's request for a "view" of 49 Revere Street and the prerelease center at 79 Chandler before the attorneys' opening statements.

A view of the locations featured in the case meant the jurors would be loaded onto a Greyhound bus and taken the short distance from the courthouse through the narrow cobblestoned streets of Beacon Hill and then the South End of Boston. At the two sites, they would be ushered from the bus to view the scenes later referenced in the upcoming trial. No questions could be asked and no comments made other than pointing out locations or items of interest. The distance between the scene of the rape and the time it took to get to the Brooke House was crucial to the Commonwealth's case.

It was a chilly winter day, with the thermometer hovering five degrees north of freezing. The cold was accompanied by periodic gusts of wind that made the temperature seem even lower than the reading on the thermometer. The group from the courthouse walked single file down the three steps from the warmth of the Greyhound and huddled together in a collective circle of shivers beneath the rusted iron ladder.

"Ladies and gentlemen, I would like you to note the rear of this apartment building, which is 49 Revere Street. This is the fire escape that the Commonwealth will prove was the means of access to the fourth floor where the victim was attacked," the prosecutor told the jury as they looked on skeptically.

"That bottom rung looks a hell of a lot higher now than it did the last time I was here," the detective with the dark eyes whispered.

As Rose spoke, one of the taller male jurors reached up unconvincingly with his right hand in a vain attempt to touch the crusted piece of iron. The juror followed up with a short tiptoed jump that fell well short of reaching his goal. Pina's lawyer opportunistically shook his head from side to side as two of the jurors mimicked his head motion.

The case was quickly slipping away in the first moments of the trial.

You had to admire Reggie Rose. Without a word, he casually and politely pushed his way through the jurors encircling the fire escape and with a two-step running start before Pina's lawyer could object, leaped as high as his five-foot-nine-inch frame would allow. He grasped the bottom rung in a death grip and arm-curled his body up onto the fire escape. Once his footing was set, he smiled down at the doubting Thomases now gasping in openmouthed admiration beneath him.

Even John Paul let loose with a modest but dignified nod of his head.

Trials were won or lost for many different reasons.

The remainder of the bus tour was uneventful, as the Greyhound traced the route from Revere Street to the Brooke House on Chandler Street. After the display at the fire escape, you knew that if Rose told the jurors he made the run in twelve minutes, they would believe him.

THE TRIAL OF LOUIS PINA

It wasn't a particularly long trial.

The primary issue would be the identity of Holly's attacker.

Before the start of the case, the defendant's attorney had moved to suppress the *Amadeus* tickets, alleging that Pina had a reasonable expectation of privacy in the contents of his wallet left at the Brooke House. Judge John Paul didn't agree, concluding no search warrant was required because Pina had a lower expectation of privacy in a halfway house setting, where all residents were subject to a search at any time.

The tickets to *Amadeus* were coming into evidence.

The four-day fray included the view of the scene, both sides' opening statements, the testimony of six witnesses, and closing arguments—a short interval in time that would determine the future life status of two polar opposites, the victim and the defendant. The legal contest was a daily walk on a tightrope of taut barbed wire suspended precariously between guilt and innocence.

One slip and all was lost.

In every rape case, Burke always called the victim as his first witness. Holly calmly took the stand, as well as the oath, and in the first hour following the parties' opening statements, she explained to the jury what had happened to her three years earlier. She carefully described the layout of her apartment, the kitchen window near the fire escape, and the *Amadeus* tickets that were missing from her nightstand and that she never got to see play. It was painful to listen to her speak about the multiple rapes and the beating she endured.

She was a compelling witness.

Holly was explaining to the jury how her assailant initially used her blouse to cover his face and then wrapped it around her eyes when the judge asked her to pause. As was his custom, His Honor called for the morning recess and reluctantly sent the jury upstairs for their daily dose of coffee and donuts. Burke sensed they didn't want to leave.

The twelve jurors and two alternates were led by a court officer to the jury room located one flight above the courtroom as both sides retreated outside. It was just after eleven in the morning as the prosecutor, detective, and victim stood in the foyer outside courtroom 808.

Holly was the first to speak.

"I know I told you both I didn't think I could identify the person who raped me," she said in a halting voice. "There were a few seconds before he put my blouse over my eyes, so I had a chance to see his face. Now that I'm here on the stand staring at him, I know it's him."

There was this split second of both exhilaration and panic as Burke tried to determine his next move. He had already told the jurors in his opening that the victim was unable to identify her attacker. Now, he was changing course midstream. Cases were won or lost on the lawyer's credibility with the jury.

"So what do you think you should do?" Rose asked as the large court officer signaled for the parties to return to courtroom 808.

A weak, "I don't know, Reggie," was the best Burke could offer as the swinging doors closed behind the trio with a thud. The prosecutor waited for Holly to resume the stand and then went to his usual position at the end of the jury enclosure next to the defense table. There was a period of hesitation as he formulated his question, and then he instinctively knew what to do. He slowly turned to face Holly and began to speak.

"Now based on the brief time that the person was in your room without your blouse covering his face, did you have a chance to look at this gentleman seated right here?" Burke said while pointing at the defendant.

There was no objection from Pina's lawyer.

"Yes, sir." Holly stared at Pina and began to nod her head up and down.

"Based on the observations you made during that limited time, can you tell this jury whether this is the same person who was in your apartment that particular night?"

The scale held in balance by Lady Justice was about to tip in the direction of the Commonwealth at that moment, but before Holly could answer, Laymon rose. He objected in full voice and requested a sidebar conference.

John Paul wanted to know why the sudden change in testimony.

"The witness told me during the recess that after seeing the defendant while testifying she is now able to identify Pina as her attacker," Burke told His Honor.

"You may have the question," the man in the black robe said brusquely, overruling defense counsel's objection.

In each case, lawyers make decisions. Burke was certain the jury knew Holly was about to identify Pina before Laymon's objection. Despite the judge's ruling, he couldn't risk being overturned on appeal if he was wrong. For all she had suffered, he couldn't put Holly through a second trial. After returning from the sidebar to the prosecution table, Burke turned to face Reggie, then John Paul, said he had no further questions, and sat down.

Burke thought briefly of his failure to object to the question put to Frost's supervisor as a rush of fear coursed through his body.

"I hope that wasn't a mistake," he whispered to Rose, who offered no comfort.

"Yeah, me too," the detective responded flatly as Pina's attorney took the floor.

Counsel for the defense did what he could to create reasonable doubt in a brief period of cross-examination of Holly. Laymon sidestepped the possible identification of his client and then moved on. It was a good strategy. He limited the amount of time Holly had to see the perp, exposing the frailty of the tentative identification, and then he waited to see what Burke had next in line.

Chris Casner was on a mission of self-identity as she confidently strode to the witness stand, adding the element of Pina's previous presence at the scene of the crime and the means of entry through the kitchen window from the fire escape. Pina glared at the woman throughout her testimony.

Chris returned the favor.

Reggie Rose was the Commonwealth's next witness. He told the jury that Pina cut his hair and shaved his mustache shortly after Holly's rape and that the defendant arrived at the Brooke House forty-five minutes late on the night of the rape, approximately fifteen minutes after Holly said her assailant left her apartment. Rose also explained that he had been able to make the trip from Revere Street to Chandler and the Brooke House in the same period of fifteen minutes.

The detective concluded by explaining he had found two tickets to the play *Amadeus* in the defendant's wallet two years after the rape had occurred.

Rose was followed by two forensics experts who added testimony that Pina's blood type and scalp and pubic hair samples were "similar" and "consistent with," but certainly not identical to, the assailant's found at the scene.

Pina chose not to testify at his trial.

The closing arguments of the case summarized the trial in one final attempt to convince the jury of the righteousness of each advocate's side. Thirty minutes for each side to cajole the jurors into believing that their point of view was the correct one.

Laymon didn't contest the fact that a rape had occurred. He argued that the overzealous prosecution merely had the wrong man.

The defense attorney explained it was a flimsy case, with a limited opportunity to make any reliable identification, buttressed by unsatisfactory blood and hair samples that could have belonged to hundreds, if not thousands, of other potential suspects. The indictments of Louis Pina had "reasonable doubt" stamped all over them.

"You don't have to take my word for it," Attorney Laymon told the jurors. "Judge Sullivan will explain the meaning of 'reasonable doubt' for you in detail later on."

As the defense attorney finished, a familiar fear of failure overwhelmed the lawyer for the Commonwealth. In his mind he felt his words really didn't matter. There was nothing he could say to change what was already in the jurors' hearts and minds.

Burke knew the so-called scientific evidence merely got you inside the courtroom door. No jury would convict Pina simply on the notion of a conclusion of *similar* forensic evidence. Neither the blood nor hair samples found at the scene were akin to a fingerprint. Instead, the prosecutor argued, it was Pina's twisted sexual trophy that eventually became the evidentiary harpoon the defense couldn't explain, minimize, or make disappear. The *Amadeus* tickets were the direct nexus between the rapist and the fourth-floor apartment at 49 Revere Street. Hidden in a metal evidence locker for two years, secured in a manila envelope, the tickets would rise like a phoenix to link Pina to his past.

He argued to the jury that it was all so clear. The *Amadeus* tickets were kept in Pina's wallet as a daily reminder of his sexual conquest, a keepsake of his wanton brutality that only a rapist could appreciate. The prosecutor searched the jurors' faces for the moment of recognition that they, *at least one of them*, understood. Instead, they stared back impassively, arms crossed, blankly looking as though he were speaking another language.

When Burke was done, he knew all was lost.

The jury would be out for three days.

SEVENTEEN

It was barely a week after the verdict on the Louis Pina trial, but in his mind, Holly's case somehow seemed a memory from the distant past. Life ebbed and flowed outside Quincy Market, as one chapter of the lawyer's life ended and another was about to begin.

Burke first met Ruth at the scheduled time of her appointment in late March, 1986. It was precisely 4:30 in the afternoon. The windy change in weather had turned the chill and frost of winter to a near sixty-degree balmy day.

So many years later, he would remember their initial meeting so clearly.

"The Power of Love" by Huey Lewis and the News was playing on a nearby radio as the frail black woman with the sad brown eyes sat with the lawyer in the conference room of his new office.

"Seventeen is my favorite number," she told him.

Maybe he imagined it, but there was a sense of the Deep South about her. Stooped by the weight of her life, she studied the scene around her slowly, nodding with approval at the exposed brick and thick chiseled beams on the fourth floor of Faneuil Hall's North Market building.

Burke's office was located a few doors from Durgin Park restaurant, and the smell of freshly baked cinnamon rolls and a hint of freshly brewed coffee percolated through the partially opened window as the two charted the course of their initial conversation.

"Seventeen?"

"Yes, seventeen. You're the seventeenth lawyer I've met with on my son Lonnie's case. I woke up this morning and said, 'The Good Lord's gonna help me to smile this day.' I could feel it in my soul. I knew it because you make number seventeen."

There was a presence to the woman, a quiet dignity that drew the listener into her story of loss. She wore the kind of yellow print flowered dress you would expect for someone who was going to church services that afternoon. Ruth quietly explained that her thirteen-year-old son had died at Children's Hospital more than two years earlier.

"None of the other sixteen lawyers were interested in representing you?" Burke asked the woman.

"The first one was, but he had another case that took up all of his time. It had something to do with pesticides poisoning some families in Woburn. He told me he couldn't represent me anymore. So I've spent all this time looking for another lawyer to help me. None of them think I have any chance to win."

"Is that the only reason?"

"No," Ruth said, hesitating before she explained.

"I think some of them were concerned about taking the case because my son's father is in jail."

"Can I ask you what he was convicted of?" Burke asked.

"Murder," Ruth said as she instinctively reached for the crucifix suspended from her neck.

There was a pause as Burke studied her face. As a prosecutor he had never had to deal with the consequence of the loss of a father or husband imprisoned for life. His focus had always been the victims of crime. There was never a thought given about what happened to the other side's family when he was convicted. For the first time, Burke realized the defendant's family members were also collateral victims of the crime. They also paid a price.

"But I've never even done a medical malpractice case before. I just left the DA's office," Burke admitted as he carefully placed the elbows of his blue button-down shirt on top of the polished oaken table.

"I know that, dear. That's why I'm here," Ruth said with enough confidence for both of them.

"I'm not sure I understand."

"Last week, I read about that poor girl on Beacon Hill that was raped and how you won her case. That's when I knew *you* were the lawyer for my Lonnie's case."

"But how do you think I can help you?"

"I want to know the truth. I need you to tell me what happened to my son. He was just thirteen," the woman said as she clutched a laced handkerchief from her worn purse and softly began to cry.

"But you're talking about Children's Hospital. It's one of the best medical facilities in the world. Nobody sues Children's Hospital," Burke interjected, sounding strangely similar to the other sixteen attorneys.

"I know that, but my Lonnie didn't need to die. The doctors told me the medication he was taking affected his liver. He was in the hospital for just a couple of days, and then he went into a coma. Three days later he was gone," Ruth said, unconsciously reaching for the cross again.

She held it between her thin fingers and stiffened her resolve to finish the story.

"I'm so sorry," Burke said as he felt the knot in his throat begin to thicken.

"I was there when my Lonnie was born and took his first breath, and I was holding his hand when he took his last. I knelt beside his bed at the hospital and prayed to the Good Lord to take me, but He took my son to be with Him instead."

It was a moment of consuming grief as Ruth described the loss of her child.

"I haven't heard the birds sing since my son left me," she told Burke as he reached toward his eyes and then instinctively pulled his hand back.

"I really don't know what to tell you. I'd like to help you, but I'm not really—"

"Do you believe in God?" the woman with the sad eyes interrupted.

"Why sure, I guess. Why?" Burke answered without conviction or an expression of faith.

"Because I know I'm here for a reason. In my heart, I believe God sent me here. Not just for me, or for my family, or even for my Lonnie, but maybe for you too. Everything happens for a reason. Nothing in life is random. Maybe you'll understand someday." Ruth reached to touch the lawyer's hand and softly added, "Please take my son's case."

MRS. FRIZZI

Burke wasn't certain why, but he made the decision to take Ruth's case shortly before she left his office on the first day they met. She smiled, laughed, and cried all in the same moment. The next morning he called her to schedule a second appointment for the following week.

The conference room on the fourth floor of the lawyer's office had a broad glass-paneled entry and three adjoining brick walls that had withstood over two hundred years of history. Meetings with clients in the conference room were off-limits to interruptions by telephone calls. The lawyer sensed this one was different as he looked up to see the receptionist place an imaginary phone to her ear and simultaneously point to him with her other hand.

"Excuse me, Ruth," Burke said to the woman with the sad brown eyes. "I need to take this phone call."

"That's OK, darlin', I got no other place to go," the client told her new lawyer.

There was a sense of calm, an inner serenity to the woman that the attorney wished he could duplicate. Any possibility of tranquility was disrupted on a daily basis by the needs of his clients. It was all so new to him, this practice of law. Burke briefly smiled at Ruth and headed to his desk to take the call. He never quite knew what to expect in moments like this.

"Hey, Tim, it's Drew. I've got a little problem," the caller explained with a note of anxiety in his voice. "I need to see you right away."

"OK, how soon can you get over here?"

"Well, I'm just around the corner at Durgin Park. It's kinda important."

"All right, I'm just finishing up with a client. I'll see you as soon as I'm done," Burke said as he ended the call and returned to his client.

The purpose of the meeting that day was to review Lonnie's medical records. It was a difficult process to follow the timeline leading up to the death of a child. His last days were all there in black-and-white, in an hour-by-hour, day-by-day handwritten recitation of attending nurses' and doctors' notes, culminating in the loss of a mother's son.

Ruth was leaving the office just as Drew was getting off the elevator and heading for the oak-and-glass front door.

"Are you going to see *my* lawyer?" the woman asked the stranger with a proud sense of ownership.

"Why yes, I am." The large trooper smiled in mild surprise.

"Well, then, I'll say a prayer for you." Ruth smiled in response.

"Thank you, ma'am, I may just need it," Drew told her as the elevators closed, ending the conversation.

There weren't many times when the trooper with the ponytail ever requested help. Fiercely independent, he never needed or asked for anyone's assistance.

This time was different.

"Do you remember when you told me you needed more business?" Drew asked his friend.

"Yeah, I do," Burke responded blankly.

"Well, I just got sued, and I need a lawyer. Know any good ones that don't cost much money?" the trooper said with a forced smile.

"Cheap lawyers aren't good, and good lawyers aren't cheap, Drew." The attorney smiled back.

"That's good to hear because now you got me for a client. It's a civil rights suit brought by the wife of a local mob hit man, Guy Frizzi. It seems *Mrs.* Frizzi was on a TWA flight out of Logan Airport to Naples, Italy. Unfortunately, the tickets she was using were stolen. I wound up arresting her and taking her off the plane. So now she's suing me for false arrest, saying that I didn't have probable cause to lock her up."

"Well, good, bad, or indifferent, you'll have the honor of being one of my first clients. I'll win your case," the newly minted civil attorney responded with a rare aura of self-confidence.

"You kidding me?"

"Nope."

For the first time, Burke didn't regret the promise he made to his friend and newest client.

CRICKETS

The bar at Crickets restaurant was nothing special, but Burke liked it. Named after the six-legged creature adorning the cupola on top of the Faneuil Hall building, the trendy watering hole was set kitty-cornered to his new office on the north side of the marketplace. The place had exposed brick walls and wooden beams encased by a three-sided glass solarium with tiny white decorator lights wrapped daintily around the palmetto palms and Ficus trees.

Even in the middle of winter, Crickets seemed almost tropical.

Burke had gotten a call from a familiar voice earlier that morning to meet for lunch on a dank, raw, and windy day in late March, 1986.

Tall, with dark hair and eyes, the man on the phone was wearing his usual jeans, black leather waistcoat, and alligator-skin cowboy boots, much to the dismay of his supervisors and in high contrast to the traditional French and Electric Blue uniform of the Massachusetts State Police.

Overhead, Jimmy Buffett sang about cheeseburgers in paradise.

"Hey, Drew," Burke began as he rose to shake his friend's large mitt. "Did you ever give Mrs. Frizzi back her plane tickets to Italy?"

"Very funny, and no, I didn't. She keeps calling all the time, wondering what we're going to do with them. I told her we have to keep them as evidence for the civil rights case she sued me on," the large trooper volleyed back.

"Well, we've had a lot worse cases than Mrs. Frizzi's," Burke offered.

"How's the biz?" Drew wanted to know as he reached for a menu with a large smiling grasshopper on the front page.

"It's goin' great. Even better than I expected. I got my first medical malpractice case the other day. It's a woman whose son died at Children's Hospital from an allergic reaction to Dilantin," the lawyer began.

"Yeah, I think I met her the other day coming out of your office. An older black woman, right?"

"Right, I really like her. She's had a tough life. Her husband's in jail for murder, and nobody else would take her case," Burke explained while scanning his menu.

"Hey, I'm sorry about the kid, but nobody sues Children's Hospital, and besides, what the hell do you know about medical malpractice cases?"

"Not much now, but I will. In some ways it's like doing one of our homicide cases. Ya know, trying to figure things out from different pieces of evidence and information, medical records, autopsies, stuff like that."

"You're friggin' nuts. You know that?" His friend smiled.

"Yeah, I think you told me that once or twice before," Burke said as both men nodded in sync and ordered french fries, a couple of quarter-pounders with cheese, and a big kosher pickle.

There was a pause in the flow as Drew's face got this quizzical, pursed-lip, raised-eyebrow expression. His head swayed from side to side in measured beat with the parrot head singing in the background.

"OK, so are you going to tell me how you got that jury to come back with a guilty on Louis Pina's case?"

"All I know is a group of the jurors came to my office the day after the verdict and gave me this," the former prosecutor explained as he handed his friend a clear six-inch piece of Lucite with a single word printed within it.

"The jury did that?"

"Yeah, they did."

"What the hell is it?"

"It's a paperweight with the word *Amadeus* laser printed inside it," Burke explained.

"What's *Amadeus* mean?"

"It means 'the love of God.'"

"Probably had something to do with the case, right?"

"Yeah, it did, Drew. Everything."

The trooper just nodded and got the kind of look on his face that indicated he wanted to say something important—the kind of message that could make a difference to someone who seldom listened to anyone else's opinion.

Drew made eye contact before he spoke.

"Well, that part of your career is over with. It's time to move on, time for you to put all these rapes and murders behind you. You need to head in a different direction."

"Yeah, I know, but I feel like every time I start to leave, something pulls me back into it again. Like there's no escaping the past."

COOK'S BRIDGE

A document called a "complaint" is the means by which a plaintiff initiates a civil lawsuit against another party. What's contained in the complaint is governed by the Massachusetts Rules of Civil Procedure. The document has to include the parties' names and addresses, the basis for the court's jurisdiction, the "counts" or allegations stated in block paragraph form, together with the "prayers" for judicial relief and a request for a jury trial.

A $120 fee is paid at the time of the filing. The clerk then issues a summons together with a copy of the complaint for a process server to deliver to the named defendant either in hand or at their last and usual residence. The defendant has twenty days to file an answer to the complaint once service has been made.

It was Burke's first civil lawsuit on behalf of a plaintiff as well as his first medical malpractice claim. It had taken weeks to review and digest the mounds of medical records in the case and then draft the factual summary. When it was finally completed, Ruth signed the complaint as the administrator of Lonnie's estate.

Unwilling to accept the reliability of the United States Postal Service, the pair walked the multipage document from Faneuil Hall to the clerk's office. It was filed with the Suffolk County clerk on the morning of October 20, 1986, ten days before the three-year statute of limitations ran out.

The leaves of the maple trees on the Boston Common had turned a twist of red-orange. Overhead, a flock of Canada geese formed a raucous V-shaped wedge as they made their way south for the winter months. There was magic in the Boston air. The Red Sox had taken an early two-game lead over the New York Mets in their first World Series appearance since 1975. Game three was to be played at Fenway the following night.

"Are you a Red Sox fan?" Burke asked Ruth as they left the courthouse in Pemberton Square.

"I don't really pay that much attention, Timmy. Just seems like I have too many other things to deal with."

"Well, this time we're going to win the World Series. It's been almost sixty-five years since the last time the Red Sox won," Burke said enthusiastically.

"That would be nice." Ruth nodded politely as she glanced up toward the blue-white mottled sky, pausing for the moment to listen to the sounds of the geese. She smiled broadly as though temporarily freed from an unspoken worry and then turned to her lawyer.

"I'd like you to come to my house and meet my family. I've told them so much about you and how you're going to help us."

"I-I normally don't do that, Ruth," Burke said stiffly, attempting to maintain a professional distance from his client.

"I don't mean this week. I know you probably want to watch the baseball games."

"Ah," was the most he could get out before he was interrupted.

"Is it because we're black?" Ruth asked.

"Of course not," Burke said defensively and perhaps too quickly.

"It would mean a lot to all of us," she told him as they slowly traced their steps back toward Faneuil Hall.

*****

Named after Captain Robert Cook, a former comb maker and officer in the colonial militia, the Cook's Bridge housing project was located on the outskirts of the town of Needham, a pleasant suburb west of Boston. The project was a series of clapboarded, cream-colored homes encircling a horseshoe-shaped one-way road. It was remotely tucked into a glacial rock outcropping that bordered an abandoned rail line, nearby Route 9, and a looming twelve-hundred-foot tall television antenna. The modest units were a flagging attempt to provide low- to moderate-income families a home. Number 33 was a cramped, three-bedroom space that housed Burke's favorite client and her remaining children.

"Here he is, everyone," Ruth announced to her family as the lawyer approached the partially opened storm door.

The smell of country-fried steak and mashed sweet potatoes and the sounds of Dick Stockton's voice giving the Mets lineup simultaneously surrounded Burke as he stepped inside the doorframe.

"I hope you're hungry. We've got the game on too," she told him while gesturing toward the living room.

"Are you my mom's lawyer?" another voice asked.

"Yes, I am," Burke said as he glanced down.

"This is my daughter Sandra," Ruth cooed as she gestured to the teen in the wheelchair. "She can sing like a bird, like a beautiful songbird."

In all of their conversations, she had never mentioned Sandra's condition. Burke thought he knew, understood, the full extent of the weight of Ruth's life.

He had no idea.

He really had no idea.

It would take four more years for her case to reach finality.

OFFER OF PROOF

Massachusetts is among a minority of states with a statute designed to protect doctors and hospitals from frivolous lawsuits. The Bay State is home to numerous hospitals, ranging in size from community and rural facilities to large urban and teaching medical schools with some of the best research facilities in the world. Following the aftermath of a medical malpractice insurance crisis in 1975, the Massachusetts legislature passed a law to screen out meritless claims of negligence.

The statute is intended to prevent members of the medical profession from being subjected to the time and expense of defending unnecessary claims of malpractice. It requires plaintiffs to present their claims to a tribunal for review before going on to trial. The rule appears in a set of forest-green-colored books known as the Massachusetts General Laws, where each category is broken into chapters and sections and given the prefixing abbreviation of "MGL."

MGL chapter 231, section 60B, requires each plaintiff to specify the factual basis of their allegations with exhibits and supporting case law to a three-member panel called a medical malpractice tribunal. The tribunal consists of a lawyer, a superior court judge, and a physician in the same specialty as the defendant doctor, all chosen at random. The trio reviews the proposed evidence and makes a threshold decision whether there is a sufficient basis for the case to continue.

The tribunal acts as a screening body and determines whether "the evidence presented is sufficient to raise a legitimate question of liability appropriate for judicial inquiry or whether the plaintiff's case is merely an unfortunate medical result."

If the tribunal majority finds for the plaintiff, the parties complete the discovery process. If the tribunal finds for the defendant, the plaintiff must post a surety bond to cover the costs of the lawsuit before they can continue further. If no bond is posted, the plaintiff's claim is dismissed with prejudice.

By statute, the Massachusetts tribunal hearing is supposed to occur within fifteen days of a defendant's response to the plaintiff's complaint. It took five months for the tribunal hearing to be scheduled after Burke received the answer from the attorneys for the defendants in Ruth's case.

It was a Friday in late March, 1987, with a foggy start to a sixty-two-degree day. The pair made their way up the broad brick stairway past Boston's city hall toward the courthouse. A chilly northeast breeze off the Atlantic pushed them forward. Coming home wouldn't be as easy.

"I don't have the money for the bond if we don't get past the tribunal," Ruth told her lawyer.

"You won't have to worry about that. We have a good shot. Try not to worry," he told her with a sense of unfulfilled bravado that belied his own insecurity.

"I know you want to help us, darlin', but if the judge thinks we don't have a case, then that should be the end of it. I don't want my kids thinking there's something here that isn't going to happen. They've all been disappointed so much before. I don't think we could take the thought of losing this case."

"OK," Burke responded blankly as they made their way up the brick steps.

Courtroom 313 was a civil session on the third floor of the courthouse and a cookie-cutter of the three others on each corner of the cold concrete building. It was also the same courtroom where the Frost case had been tried. You never knew which room you were in unless you read the sign above the courtroom doors or knew from which direction the sun poured into the barren twelve-paneled windows. It was a different side of the law equation for the former prosecutor, but the rush of adrenaline to his brain and the fear of failure were exactly the same.

"I've read your materials, Mr. Burke. Perhaps you can enlighten the panel why this isn't simply an unfortunate medical result," the man in the black robe asked as the defendant's lawyer nodded in obvious agreement.

There was an edge to the judge's voice, a challenging tone that signified he had already made up his mind.

"There are a host of reasons, Your Honor. There were classic symptoms of an allergic reaction present in this case that should have been apparent to any practicing physician. My client's son had lost ten percent of his body weight in less than a month after taking this medication. He was lethargic, complained of constant abdominal pain, and had developed a fine rash over his face and most of the trunk of his body. Rather than take him off the Dilantin, his doctor encouraged his mother to continue with the medication, assuring her that her son Lonnie would be fine. The failure to take him off this medication worsened an already desperate situation. Although he was severely jaundiced and barely able to stand, he was denied admission to Children's Hospital on several occasions despite the obvious evidence of a drug fever. His liver was rendered essentially dysfunctional from the Dilantin. When Lonnie was finally admitted, he was left unattended and fell against the wall in his room, suffering brain trauma that resulted in him lapsing into a coma. He died three days later."

There was an audible gasp from the front row of the gallery as Ruth relived her moment of loss.

"This child should never have died," Burke said softly and turned to see her raise a lace-edged handkerchief to her eyes.

There was silence from the members of the panel as they each surveyed Burke for what seemed an eternity. He waited for their questions, which never came, and he knew he had failed. A rush of heat overcame him as his face flushed and the room began to slowly drift around him.

"We'll hear from counsel for the defense," he heard the judge say along with something about taking a seat.

When the hearing was done, Burke rose from the leather cushioned chair and headed for the swinging doors at the back of the courtroom.

SIR CHARLES

Burke met a whole lot of lawyers in the biz. Most were forgettable, unremarkable throwaways. He passed time with them only because they happened, by circumstance or cosmic design, to be on the other side of his case. Born or bred into a culture of ego and pseudointellectual pursuit, too many were preening, self-serving stiffs.

That wasn't true about the defense attorney for the premier medical facility in New England. There was a regal appearance about the man. He was a Jimmy Stewart knockoff with a worn leather briefcase.

"So what the hell are *you* doing in a medical malpractice case, kid?" Charlie Dunn bellowed to the junior lawyer outside courtroom 313. "You're a little out of your element, don't you think? This ain't no murder case, ya know."

"I know that, Mr. Dunn," Burke said hesitantly as he smiled faintly at the lawyer representing Children's Hospital.

"Who the hell you calling Mr. Dunn? That's my father's name. It's Charlie," the prematurely gray-haired man said as he extended his right hand to his opponent.

He had a runner's build, skinny, with elongated calves and thighs, fine-boned hands, and matching thin fingers. Dunn had grown up in the West End of Boston. He spent his early years playing baseball and boxing for the West End House until he was fourteen. He then spent the next two years in a sanatorium after being stricken with infectious tuberculosis. Bedridden in an isolation unit for six months, he took fifty-two pills a day for the cure. It was a lonely time, and he was given to bouts of depression and introspection. Perseverance, antibiotics, and an unbreakable will purged the thick mucus from his lungs and left him driven to make up for lost time.

"OK, Mr. Dunn, er, Charlie," Burke responded.

"You done good for your client today. Don't pay any attention to that old fart on the bench. A judge is just some lawyer that knew the governor. That guy couldn't try a case if he had a roadmap, a ten-dollar compass, and a cigar store Indian for a guide."

"Thanks," Burke mustered as he headed for the bank of elevators.

It wasn't instantaneous, but he liked the lawyer on the other side of Ruth's case. Charlie Dunn was brash and confident. He was someone who had tried a million medical malpractice cases and felt comfortable in his arena. Burke was the outsider, the interloper with no experience. For the first time he felt intimidated by the opposition.

"How do you think we did today?" Ruth asked quietly inside the confines of the elevator.

"We did fine, I guess," Burke responded with a calculated measure of uncertainty and self-doubt.

CHILDREN'S HOSPITAL

Children's Hospital provides an incredible array of medical treatment for its patients. From life-saving neonatal care for newborns to breakthrough treatments for young adults with cancer, Children's reputation within the Boston medical community, indeed the country, was unmatched.

There were moments when Burke regretted his decision to bring the lawsuit against the hospital. He found himself in awe of the doctors working there, feeling inferior to their intellect, their knowledge of medicine, and their understanding of life's course. He never told Ruth of these thoughts, as he struggled with his own internal notion of right and wrong, pitted against the need to protect a single mother whose vain attempt to save her son had failed. Burke feared the looming likelihood of his own failure for the woman who had blindly entrusted her case to him.

In reality, he felt the doctors who had prescribed Dilantin and then failed to diagnose the allergic reaction played a far more significant role in Lonnie's death than the hospital. It was their individual responsibility he would have to establish to a jury. Before the tribunal hearing the lawyer added both their names as parties to the complaint, as well as the attending physician at Children's who refused to admit Lonnie.

It had been over a week since the hearing in courtroom 313.

"I just got word from the court on our offer of proof," Burke explained to his client over the telephone.

"Oh please, Lord, tell me they allowed it."

"They did, Ruth. The tribunal found a legitimate basis in our proof allowing us to continue with the lawsuit against all the defendants."

Burke felt a mixture of elation and dread as a result of the decision—elation that the panel found merit in the evidence he had assembled, and dread that the preliminary decision was merely postponing the inevitable verdict against his client's case.

"Oh, Lordy, I have the best lawyer in Boston representing me," Ruth proclaimed for all of her family gathered by her side to hear.

"It's just a first step. We have a long way to go, Ruth." Burke tried to temper the moment as he listened to the sounds of happy voices all asking what it meant.

"Oh, I know, I know, but it just makes me feel like we have a chance."

"We do, but it's going to be a long, difficult case."

There was a brief pause as he could hear Ruth clear her throat.

"Timmy, no matter what happens, I just want to say thank you for believing in my Lonnie's case."

DILANTIN

Months passed into years as the malpractice case dragged on in a seemingly endless series of motions and requests for discovery between the plaintiff and the defendants. With each round of information exchanged, Burke gradually learned more about his case and the cause of Lonnie's untimely death. He shared each bit of new information with his client, who would in most instances silently nod her head and close her eyes without responding. There were moments when he hesitated to relate any news that he knew would only bring more pain to Ruth.

As was their custom, the lawyer and his client frequently met in his office to discuss the case and, as time wore on, their lives.

Dilantin is an anticonvulsant medication normally prescribed to epileptic patients to prevent seizures. While neutral in outward appearance, Dilantin is an unwittingly racist drug. For some unknown reason, a significantly larger percentage of blacks are allergic to Dilantin than whites.

The symptoms of swollen glands, fever, jaundice, lethargy, weight loss, and rash appear one to six weeks after ingestion of the medication. The course of an allergic reaction to Dilantin has been either that of complete recovery after withdrawal from the drug and steroid therapy or severe hepatic necrosis resulting in the death of the patient. In a medical study conducted in the early eighties, death was the result of a hypersensitivity to Dilantin in several cases, all of them due to liver failure.

Lonnie was one of the unfortunate few.

"I thought I was being a good mother. When we moved out of Boston, I enrolled Lonnie in a mostly white school. I wanted him to be able to do well in his classes, to compete with the other kids there, not just in football, but in his studies too. Do you know what I mean?"

107

Burke nodded in silent agreement.

"When he started to get headaches in class, I took him to see the doctor. He said to give him Dilantin. And that's what I did. I thought I was being a good mother. I made him take his medication every day so he would get better," Ruth said as she momentarily turned her face away.

"When he got the rash, I had my doubts, but the doctor said to keep giving it to him. So that's what I did. I just kept giving him that *damn* Dilantin."

It was the first and only time Burke ever heard Ruth use any profanity.

"Now I look back and I wonder if it was me that killed him, because I cared too much," she explained, holding back her tears.

"Ruth, you had no way of knowing."

"No, I know, I know. The Good Lord made the decision to take my Lonnie, but the thought burns my heart and my soul, each and every day."

102-104 BELLEVUE STREET

The city of Dorchester was fighting a losing battle to stem the wash of drugs infesting its streets. The problem frequently began with a single boarded-up house being used to sell drugs. Soon the infection spread the length of the street and then eventually to a block, until an entire neighborhood fell prey to the blight and devastation of wanton drug sales. The area surrounding Bellevue Street was on the downhill slide of an epidemic of cocaine.

The ramshackle three-story apartment building at 102–104 Bellevue Street contained six units, set back from a roadway, and several British-made Sterlings were frequently parked nearby. The cars were safe from theft, patiently waiting for their owners to return with rolls of cash made from the cocaine they sold inside.

Located just minutes from the scene of the triple homicide at Jacobs Street, 102–104 Bellevue presented a flurry of day-to-day foot traffic that stretched from the street to the front doorway of the dilapidated, gray, asbestos-shingled structure.

Interestingly, the front door of the run-down building was equipped with a recently installed state-of-the-art security system, preventing unwanted entry without permission from one of the tenants living within. The buzzer system had been wired to all the apartments in the building, including the unheated three-room dump on the top floor. There was no elevator, just a brisk three-story climb to the top floor of the building, where you could buy a temporary, drug-induced suspended sentence from the miseries of your life.

The narrow hallway on the third floor provided just enough space for a single person to pass down the corridor toward the recently installed blue steel door. There was no doorknob. A slab of hardened metal was welded over the area where the door handle should have been. The door was Stanley's best exterior model, with reinforced side panels, a custom dead bolt, and a peephole placed at eye level. Beneath the beveled glass of the peephole was a larger, drilled-out pass-through hole, designed for money to be passed into the apartment and drugs to be sent back out. Inside, the unidentified dealer remained secure, never to be seen by the anxious buyer.

On the other side of the steel door, a single chair, three worn snow tires, and a seemingly endless supply of old pizza boxes and takeout bags from local eateries littered the otherwise empty interior of the three-room apartment. Two matching three-foot-long two-by-fours placed into heavy L-shaped metal brackets braced the door and protected the dealers inside from rip-offs. You would need a sledgehammer to take the fortified door down.

A .45-caliber automatic was kept next to the door, just in case.

Albert Lewin was born in Jamaica. Tall and junkie-thin, Lewin and some friends spent countless hours in the unheated apartment on Bellevue Street. The Jamaicans averaged a couple grand each day dealing coke out of the third-floor apartment. No one seemed to mind, let alone notice.

Carlos Luna was a Boston police officer assigned to the department's drug unit. Short and squat with curly dark hair, Luna had been a cop for years, maybe too many. On a gray day in midwinter, Carlos Luna applied for a warrant to search the drug house on Bellevue Street, claiming in his affidavit that a confidential informant told him a "short Hispanic male" named Stevie1 was selling cocaine on the third floor.

In the body of the affidavit, Luna explained how he followed up on the informant's lead, claiming he had personally bought cocaine at the apartment on two separate occasions in the middle of February. Luna swore to a magistrate under the pains and penalties of perjury that the information contained in the affidavit was true. The search warrant for 102–104 Bellevue Street was issued, and plans were made by members of the Boston police drug unit to take the dealers down the following day.

On February 17, 1988, one of several .45-caliber bullets fired from inside the unfurnished apartment ripped through the Stanley steel door and into the forehead of Boston police officer Sherman Griffiths as he struck the door with a sledgehammer. The unidentified shooter fled undetected down the back stairs of the apartment as other members of the drug unit struggled to recover the wounded officer's body from the narrow hallway.

They were unable to break down the reinforced steel door.

Subsequent investigation revealed that Luna had made several material misrepresentations in his affidavit for the search warrant for Bellevue Street. Although Luna claimed he personally made the drug buys on the third floor, it was later learned they were made by two other confidential informants, clearly not Luna and certainly not in his presence.

Luna had never spoken to the original confidential informant mentioned in his affidavit. Luna learned about Bellevue Street from another police officer who told him about the drug house. In his affidavit, Luna said he witnessed unusual foot traffic to the apartment and other transactions at the scene. Although there was plenty of foot traffic in and out of the drug house, there was real doubt if Luna had ever previously been to Bellevue Street.

Albert Lewin was subsequently arrested for the murder of Sherman Griffiths. Much of the evidence seized at the murder scene was later ruled inadmissible following a motion to suppress hearing and appeal to the Supreme Judicial Court. The court ruled Luna falsified his original affidavit and the homicide detectives had failed to obtain a search warrant for the crime scene.

At the request of Lewin's attorneys, his trial was transferred to the western part of Massachusetts due to local adverse pretrial publicity. The Commonwealth's case against Albert Lewin was further undermined, in part, by Luna's testimony at trial that his superiors and a prosecutor encouraged him to fabricate a nonexistent informant. The only physical evidence linking Lewin to the murder weapon was a partial fingerprint on the .45 automatic, discovered some thirty months after the shooting. The delay in discovery only fueled more questions by the defense, challenging the authenticity of the print.

Lewin's case was also bolstered by the testimony of an MIT scientist who had previously helped the FBI develop the process for determining the presence of gunshot primer residue on swabs taken from a suspect's hands. Boston police tested Lewin's hands the night Griffiths was shot, and the defense expert opined it was impossible for Lewin to have fired the weapon. His testimony was offset by an FBI agent who found gunshot residue on both cuffs of the sweatshirt worn by the suspect the night of the shooting, but the prosecution expert was unable to conclusively conclude Lewin had fired the murder weapon.

A jury summarily acquitted the thirty-four-year-old Jamaican after less than four hours of deliberation.

Carlos Luna was subsequently indicted for filing false police reports and perjury. He was convicted and sentenced to five years probation. He ultimately resigned from the Boston Police Department.

PREMISES LIABILITY

It was a blind call to Burke's office on the fourth floor of the North Market building. The admin didn't recognize the female voice or her name, but she put the stranger's call through nevertheless. Running a law office meant you dealt with many unknowns in the world. People in need, good or bad, you had to talk to all of them. Even if it meant you couldn't help them in the end.

The caller's voice sounded somehow saddened as the lawyer picked up the receiver and listened patiently.

"Hello, Mr. Burke? My name is Deirdre Griffiths. A mutual friend suggested that I should contact you." The caller cleared her voice at the end of the sentence and took a breath as if she were reading from a prepared script.

"My husband was murdered by a drug dealer in Dorchester not too long ago. He was a Boston police officer. His killer was acquitted by a jury because some of the evidence was suppressed." The woman's voice hardened as she explained.

"Are you talking about the Sherman Griffiths case?"

"Yes, I am Sherm's widow," the female caller said.

"I'm terribly sorry about what happened to officer Griffiths and for your loss," Burke said woodenly, momentarily struggling to say something meaningful.

"Thank you. I realize that there's nothing I can do about the person who killed Sherman, but the people who owned the drug house had to know what was going on there. I'd like to meet with you and discuss the possibility of suing the owners of the house on Bellevue Street where Sherman was killed," the caller explained.

There was a brief pause as the lawyer considered the possibility of a lawsuit. There weren't many options available.

"You mean suing on some kind of premises liability theory?"

"I guess so. I mean is that possible?"

"Well, drug dealing is inherently an ultra-hazardous activity. Selling drugs usually involves guns and violence. It creates a risk of harm to anyone who happens to come near the dealers, not just the drug buyers."

"So anyone is at risk, is that what you are saying?"

"Yes, the legal theory is that if you can prove a property owner knows or has reason to know that drug selling is going on inside their property, and ignores it or even profits by it, then they should be held financially responsible for the injury or death to someone, like a police officer, who lawfully comes onto their property."

"So essentially the property owner is playing a part in the drug dealing by allowing it to happen, right?"

"Exactly, the argument is that it's *foreseeable* that someone is going to be hurt or even killed because of the owner's failure to do anything about the drug dealers, just like Sherman was. I'd have to do some research on the issue. I'm just not sure there is any precedent for this type of lawsuit."

"Can I at least come in and talk to you about the case?"

"Sure, how about tomorrow?" the attorney responded with a note of uncertainty.

The woman appeared at Burke's office early the following morning on a calm, summer day. It was surreal to listen to her dispassionately describe the murder of the Boston police officer whose trial had dominated the media for much of the previous year. The potential client was unfailingly polite and understated in the way she explained the tragedy visited upon her family. Despite the enormity of loss, there was no expression of self-pity.

Deirdre explained she had been a nurse at Children's Hospital, working in the cardiac intensive care unit when she first met her husband. Burke immediately thought of Ruth at the mention of Children's Hospital, wondering if the two women's lives had ever crossed.

"When we first met, Sherm was trying to decide if he wanted to become a pharmacist or a Boston police officer. Kind of strange about the paths we choose, isn't it?"

"Yes, it is."

Burke hesitated before he spoke again.

"You know that when I was in the DA's office, before your husband became a police officer, I prosecuted a detective from the drug unit for stealing money from a drug dealer, don't you?"

"I do. That's one of the reasons I called you. Sherm was an honest person. He would never have tolerated that. He cared too much about his work and his family to ever do anything wrong. I want people to know that."

Burke silently nodded as the quiet woman described her husband.

"Sherm was special. We dated for a couple of years, got married, and had our two girls within two years. He was a big guy, with reddish hair and a full beard. He was always happy, kind of boisterous, and just so friendly to everyone. I miss him so much," she added, closing her eyes.

There was a pause linked to the acceptance of her loss.

Deirdre Griffiths had been dealt a cruel blow by the death of her husband, worsened by the knowledge that his murderer had been set free, suffering only a summary deportation back to his native Jamaica. All that remained was the lingering question of accountability.

In her mind, it wasn't simply the drug dealer who had pulled the trigger. There were others who shared a portion of responsibility for Sherman's death, operating beneath the surface of public awareness.

"I'm sure they didn't intend for Sherman to die, but the owners of the house on Bellevue Street had to know what was going on inside their property. I can't ignore that," the young widow quietly explained to the lawyer.

There was an uncomfortable moment of hesitation as the woman looked for Burke's response. There was none forthcoming.

"I owe my husband that much. Many police marriages aren't good ones, but Sherm and I were very much in love. He was the love of my life. He absolutely adored his two daughters. He loved all of his girls, all three of us," Deirdre explained.

Burke had taught himself to bite the inside of his cheek whenever he felt the need to distance himself from the emotional ties a client brought to him. The temporary pain was a way of placing a protective barrier between his mind and that of his client. It was an invisible shield that kept him from getting too close, too involved, allowing him to stay less committed.

"I'm not sure I can help you," Burke began slowly as his teeth made the necessary chewing motion on the right side of his cheek.

"There really isn't any case law for this kind of situation. It would be very difficult to prove the landlords knew what was happening there."

"I understand," Deirdre said without hesitation as she pulled back from the conference table and looked into Burke's eyes.

She smiled, even though she wanted to cry. The lawyer's response was another disappointment, another rejection, a sense of unmeasured loss that the widow had become accustomed to.

There was the briefest of moments when Burke sensed her feeling of rejection. For some unknown reason, he thought of Ruth's words to him during their first meeting at the same table in his conference room.

Everything happens for a reason. Nothing in life is random. Maybe you'll understand someday, the frail black woman had told him.

In that moment his hesitation was gone. He sensed a need to commit to the cop's widow. There were thousands of lawyers in Boston, and she was asking only him for help. Burke couldn't explain why, but he knew misfortunes such as Deirdre's were beyond human comprehension, occurring for a reason that may never be understood.

In that moment, he became a part of her tragedy. Burke wanted to ask Deirdre if she believed in destiny and God, but he decided not to.

"I'll be happy to take your case," he told her instead.

THE ESTATE OF SHERMAN GRIFFITHS

In Massachusetts, a deceased person isn't allowed to bring a lawsuit against another party.

The deceased's estate is the party authorized to bring a claim for any injuries leading to the person's death. If the death is caused by the negligence of another person or by willful or reckless actions of that person, then the estate can recover for the deceased's reasonably expected income over the anticipated span of his or her life. The suit is called a wrongful death claim. The lawsuit is governed by MGL chapter 229, section 2, and provides for recovery of the loss of consortium or the loss of companionship as well as lost income.

The probate court normally appoints the spouse, the next of kin, or the executor specified in the deceased's will as the party to initiate the suit. Like the lawsuit filed by Ruth on behalf of her son Lonnie, such was the case with Sherman Griffiths. His wife Deirdre was appointed the executor by the probate court, authorizing her to act upon his behalf.

"So, Timothy, I understand you got a new case," Mark Newman said to his friend the day following the meeting with Deirdre Griffiths.

There was an air of enthusiasm to the question from the normally stoic lawyer from Chelsea. Although the two attorneys shared the same office space, they seldom worked cases together. This one would be different. Their history that had begun years earlier would bind them together for the next five years.

"Yeah, I told Deirdre I'd take her case. You interested in getting involved?" Burke asked, hoping his friend would agree.

Although the two had worked together in the homicide unit, Newman was later transferred to become the head of the drug unit for Suffolk County,

117

prosecuting major dealers in the Boston area, an experience invaluable to the Griffiths case.

"I thought we'd left the crime and violence behind once we were out of the DA's office."

"It doesn't seem like we've ever really been able to escape any of it, even on the civil side of the law, does it?" Burke agreed.

"It sounds strange, but I'd like to do something to make it better, somehow. Not like we're going to change the world, but at least try to make things right for Deirdre, her kids, and maybe for some of the people living there who have no hope, no chance for anything except for a world of misery, crime, and cocaine."

The comments made Burke think of Chelsea and Newman's Meat Land, wondering if that was his friend's motivation.

"So, you interested in getting involved?" Burke repeated.

"I am. I feel really bad about what happened to Deirdre's family with the killer going free, but this case isn't what we've been used to doing in the homicide unit, you know that don't you?" his new co-counsel asked.

"I know. It's going to be a hell of a lot of work to prove the landlords knew what was going on inside the third-floor apartment. Some of the cops may not want to talk to us because of the problem with the search warrant."

"It's not just some of the cops—none of the drug dealers are going to say anything either. We're going to need someone from inside the drug house to tell us what was going on behind the scenes there." Newman added quickly.

"I think the first thing we should do is draft a Freedom of Information request and see what we can learn about the investigation the Boston police conducted," Burke suggested.

"That's a good idea, but do you know any of the detectives involved in the investigation, somebody who knows what happened the night Sherman was killed?"

"Yeah, I do," Burke responded while picturing the detective with the dark, intense eyes.

"Who is it?" Newman asked.

"Reggie Rose."

FAIR INFORMATION PRACTICES ACT

Burke wasn't sure why he always referred to it as the "Freedom of Information statute." Its proper name, the Fair Information Practices Act, was contained in a series of forest green volumes encased in a three-tiered oak bookshelf adjoining his desk.

Massachusetts General Laws chapter 66, section 10, was intended to provide the public with access to official documents and to open the actions of government to unrestricted scrutiny. That access included police reports in cases that were no longer considered ongoing investigations.

The investigation of Sherman Griffiths's murder officially concluded once the jury acquitted Albert Lewin.

The file detailing the events leading to the officer's murder was a compilation of dozens of witness statements, on-scene photographs, and forensic and ballistic test results, as well as internal police memorandums.

Deirdre's civil suit against the landlords would be hamstrung without the information contained in the Boston police investigation. Shortly after the lawsuit was initiated, the two lawyers representing his widow filed the necessary motions for access to the file.

"How many requests have the Boston police denied?" Deirdre asked as the trio sat in the lawyers' conference room in Faneuil Hall.

"This makes the third time we've written to them, and each time they've refused to produce the investigative file in Sherman's case," Burke began.

"They know you're representing *me*, right? I mean it's *my* husband that was murdered. I have a right to know what happened to him, how and why he died."

"That doesn't seem to make any difference," one of the lawyers responded.

"Have they offered any reason why they won't give the file to us?" Deirdre asked with an increased sense of frustration.

"Nothing other than that they claim the file is protected from disclosure by the language of the statute." Newman explained.

"Do we have any right to appeal their decision?"

"Yes, we've done that already. It's going to be heard by the single justice of the Supreme Judicial Court. Judge Nolan is scheduled to hear it later this week." Burke added.

Joe Nolan was old-school. A strict constructionist of the United States Constitution, he understood the difference between legal theory and social engineering. Nolan provided the lone dissenting vote in the state court ruling against St. Patrick's Day parade organizers from South Boston who wanted to ban gay participation.

The Massachusetts Supreme Court's decision was appealed to the United States Supreme Court, and in an unusual 9–0 unanimous ruling, held that parades like the one in South Boston were protected forms of expression under the First Amendment. The state could not compel organizers to include groups with messages the organizers disfavored.

It was clear an unpopular decision wouldn't dissuade Nolan from doing what he thought was the right thing—the correct legal decision under the law, that is.

The highest court in the Commonwealth was located in Pemberton Square on the fifteenth floor of the "new" courthouse built in 1937. Like an aging opera house in need of repair, the appellate court was a dated architectural scheme barely two steps above the décor of the Spartan trial courtrooms several floors below. At least all the blue leather chairs matched each other and both counsel tables came equipped with their own silver pitcher for water. Burke never felt comfortable enough to check to see if there was anything in it.

The podium positioned in the middle of the justices' bench was equipped with a small replica of a traffic light, used to time the length of speaking opportunity allotted for each attorney. At the flash of the green light the advocate could begin to speak, when the yellow light flashed you had one minute left to sum up, and when the light turned red, you stopped.

Some lawyers seemed to have a problem with that concept.

MASTER PLAN

There was an ebb and flow to Burke's life that was connected to, and through, his clients. Their history and struggles often wound their way into his mind, becoming his own issues. Of them all, it was the frail black woman who had the greatest affect. Although his law practice had become stable with many different types of clients, he frequently found himself wondering how Ruth would think or react to a client or a given situation, gradually mimicking her acceptance of the things in life she knew she could never change.

"Are you religious, Timmy?" his favorite client asked as they sat in the conference room again reviewing Lonnie's medical records from Children's Hospital.

"I'm a Catholic, Ruth, but I'm not sure that makes me religious. Why?"

"I was just thinking about how I came to meet you."

"Why is that?"

Ruth looked at her lawyer and smiled warmly before she spoke.

"Because I think God brings people together for reasons we may never understand. He has a plan that only He knows about."

"How do you mean?"

"I'm not sure I ever told you this, but the reason I came to you was because of the girl who was raped in Beacon Hill. I read about her case in the newspaper—that's why I called your office. If you didn't take her case, I would never have known about you, or ever met you. So maybe something good came out of something so bad."

"I see what you mean," the lawyer responded without agreeing.

Burke leaned back in his chair and momentarily thought about his decision to leave the DA's office and the second chance he had been given to redeem himself by prosecuting Holly's case. He wondered how different his life would have been had he chosen not to.

"Nothing in life is random," Ruth told him again. "God has a plan for all of us. We just need to find our way to see it."

He looked into her brown eyes not knowing what to expect as she continued.

"You know being a lawyer is a gift to help people. You have the chance to do so much good in this world, helping people who have lost their way. You have the strength they need. God gives you the chance to make a difference for them."

Burke hesitated to tell Ruth it was because of her that he had taken Deirdre's case. Admitting it meant Burke accepted Ruth's belief in God's master plan.

The lawyer paused just long enough to decide whether to mention it.

"That's interesting to hear you say that, Ruth. I just took another case because of what you told me about people being brought together. It's a woman whose husband was killed in a drug raid. He was a Boston police officer. The killer went free. I feel like everybody has let her down."

Ruth smiled with approval at her lawyer.

"I know, darlin'. I heard about that case and how you're suing the landlords for his widow. I'm going to pray for her. We've both lost something very precious."

THE AGNOSTIC

1990 was a good year.

The Red Sox won their division, finishing twenty-one games in front of the Yankees before losing four straight to the Oakland A's in the American League playoffs. Despite their shortcomings, they were a team that, even if temporarily, gave you something to believe in.

"How is Ruth's case coming along, Timothy?" Newman asked Burke as the pair sat at the bar in Crickets, sharing a drink on a quiet Friday afternoon.

Deirdre and Ruth's cases had become a constant source of welcome conversation between the attorneys. Two women with parallel lives of loss, shepherded by men with very different backgrounds, down an uncertain and uncharted path.

"It's interesting. Ruth said something to me the other day about her belief in God. She says there's something out there, bigger than all of us, with a master plan that somehow weaves us all together amid the chaos," Burke began in an attempt to explain what he had learned from his client.

There was no immediate response from Newman, who simply stared straight ahead.

"I don't know what to think, Mark. There was a point back a couple of years ago, when we were both in the DA's office, doing all the murder cases, going to the scenes of the shootings and stabbings—I just started to have so many doubts about God and why this kind of thing happens to some people. Then when my brother and father..." Burke's voice trailed off into the background sounds of the bar.

"I don't know if anyone can explain why tragedies happen," Newman said with a simple shake of his head.

"Do *you* believe in God?" Burke blurted out as he turned to face his friend.

There was a moment of hesitation before his companion responded.

"It's just that I come from a different place, Timothy, a different view of life and the hereafter," Newman explained.

Burke had known his friend for years. They had shared every type of emotional experience during that time, and yet, he never heard Newman reveal his feelings about the topic of a higher being.

"I'm sure I did believe at one point, but I think learning about the Holocaust changed me. My parents were believers. They went to Temple in Chelsea all the time, but me, personally? I can't reconcile the murders of six million people by the Nazis with the idea of there being a God. If there were, why would He have allowed something so horrible to happen? No, I believe in people, not in religion. I think we should be good to each other because it's the right thing to do, but not because it's going to get us into heaven."

"C'mon, Mark, you don't think there's a plan out there? That we all have a destiny? That people are brought together for an unknown reason? That you have to have faith?"

"No, Timothy. Sorry, I just don't."

Burke had the greatest respect for his friend.

Newman was smart, thoughtful, loyal, and unyieldingly kind to everyone with whom he dealt. In many ways, he was a mirror image of Ruth. Burke felt torn between the beliefs of two people whose thoughts mattered to him, yet were the polar opposites of each other. At the same time, he felt a sense of his own weakness for not being able to decide about something as fundamental as the existence of God.

MOTHER LODE

Judge Nolan's decision following the hearing in the Supreme Judicial Court was brief and direct. He ordered the Boston police to immediately produce the entire investigative file for the lawyers representing Griffiths's widow.

The contents were delivered that week to their office at Faneuil Hall in two very large, heavy cardboard boxes with the name *Casey & Hayes Movers* imprinted on the sides in bold red letters.

They were a mother lode of information.

It was all there: photographs of the scene; dozens of interviews with tenants, suspects, neighbors, and detectives from the drug unit, autopsy reports; forensic and ballistic test results; and perhaps most importantly, tape-recorded interviews by the police of one of the Bellevue Street landlords, Thomas Campbell, and his electrician Michael McDonald.

"Did you happen to notice the name of the detective who did the interview of the electrician for the landlord?" Newman asked as the pair meticulously went through the reams of papers and documents piled across the conference room floor and table.

"Yeah, I did. It was Reggie Rose," Burke said as he thought of his connection to the detective, Holly Robins, Ruth, and now Deirdre.

Both men were excited about the possibilities created by the newly obtained file. The lawyers had been operating in an information vacuum, with little more than hearsay and newspaper reports to rely upon in building their case. They needed to prove exactly what the owners of the Bellevue Street apartment building knew about the presence of drug dealers on their property before the death of Sherman Griffiths. In the year preceding the trial, there hadn't been any emphasis in the press about a connection between the landlords and their Jamaican tenants. The primary storyline was the false affidavit submitted by Carlos Luna and the inevitable claim of a cover-up that followed.

"I'm sure the people at Boston police headquarters didn't want all of this being dredged up again in another lawsuit. I think that's why they tried so hard to prevent us from getting this material," Newman said to his friend.

"Take a look—the police interviewed one of the landlords. His name is Thomas Campbell. This is incredible stuff. The landlord told them he was up on the third floor personally collecting the rent in cash from the dealers. The electrician was up there all the time too, doing work. The landlord told the detectives the apartment was rented to some Jamaican guy named Delray Ferguson, but he never met him. Campbell says he saw the steel door right after it was installed, but claims he never saw the pass-through hole there," Burke added with a note of incredulity.

"The landlord says he went up there to the third floor before Sherman was shot and never sees the other hole beneath the peephole in the steel door?"

"Yes, take a look at the photograph. How do you *not* see this second hole in the door? It's got two two-by-fours behind it and no doorknob," Burke responded, pointing to another picture.

"Are you kidding me? Look at these other pictures—there's nothing inside this apartment but empty pizza boxes and old snow tires."

"Look, here's a police report about a drug raid at the same third-floor apartment in April 1987. A detective named Rubin Colon broke through the old wooden door in the apartment before they put the new steel one in with the two-by-fours."

"What'd he find?"

"He took a .38 revolver and twenty-two packets of cocaine off of one of the drug dealers inside the same apartment where Sherman was killed."

"Colon's lucky he wasn't shot. That must be why the dealers replaced the wooden door with the steel one."

"Did Campbell own the place then?"

"Yeah, he and his partner bought Bellevue Street about six weeks *before* the first police raid happened," Newman explained.

"Ya know what? I think we may just have a case here. We need to call Deirdre." Burke smiled, reaching for the phone.

THE DISCOVERY

The process of information gathering in a civil case is called "discovery." It, like other aspects of litigation, is governed by the Massachusetts Rules of Civil Procedure. The rules essentially allow each party to ask the other side thirty written questions regarding their education, marital status, employment history, issues relating to their respective legal claims or defenses and, of course, the facts of the case. These written questions are called interrogatories or "INTs" for short. Once completed, they are signed under the pains and penalties of perjury, and returned to the opposing side within thirty days from the date of their receipt.

The other tool used for obtaining documents in civil litigation is called a request for the production of documents, or "RPDs." The motion for RPDs is normally filed contemporaneously with the interrogatories and requires the production of any document of evidentiary value in the possession, custody, or control of the other party. Once discovery was completed, the lawyers set dates to take the depositions of the various witnesses and parties to the case.

Burke often wondered if Deirdre and Ruth's paths ever crossed while Lonnie was at Children's Hospital. In his mind he pictured the two women together, unknown to each other, passing in an elevator, a parking lot, the cafeteria, or more directly while the young boy was in one of the special care units near where Deirdre worked—two momentary strangers to be connected later in life through the tragedy of their respective loss. Burke wished there were a way to file a motion to reproduce the past and discover an undisclosed possible connection.

127

Despite his efforts, there was no previous interaction between his two clients. Perhaps it was enough to know the two women shared a common thread in the present.

Burke drafted the INTs and RPDs for Children's Hospital, requiring them to produce all the documents in their possession pertaining to the care and medical treatment Lonnie had received. Nurses' notes, blood tests, medications, treatment plans, doctors' orders and prescriptions, autopsy reports, tissue samples, and photographs. The list was endless.

One of the lingering unanswered questions in the young boy's case revolved around why Lonnie had fallen shortly before he lapsed into a coma.

The answer came in a one-page document randomly immersed in a sea of thousands of pages of discovery delivered to Burke's office months after the tribunal's decision on the offer of proof. Entitled "Incident Report," the nurse attending Lonnie's care the night he fell wrote the document.

"I think I know what happened that night, Ruth," Burke cautiously explained to his client.

She simultaneously placed one hand over her heart and the other over her mouth as she sat motionless, listening.

"The nurse forgot to put the bedrail up on one side of his bed. Even though he could barely walk, Lonnie was able to get out of his bed because the protective bedrail wasn't in place. He fell against the side of the wall, striking his head. That's how he got the injury to his head. After that happened, he was hemorrhaging internally—that's why he went into the coma."

Ruth's normal reaction was to nod and quietly hum to herself without speaking, which she did at that moment. She lowered her head onto her chest, closed her eyes, and slowly rocked back and forth.

"Oh my Lord, I feel so bad for that poor nurse," the frail black woman told her lawyer.

ROSA

It was less than a week before Ruth's upcoming deposition.

The Red Sox had drifted into nonfactors that year with mediocre pitching and an inconsistent lineup. Outside Burke's office, the sounds of the usual pedestrian bustle within Quincy Market drifted in and out of the partially opened windows. Summer was ebbing as the pair sat talking in the conference room of the lawyer's office, comfortable with each other it seemed from their very first meeting.

"We have the same birthday, you know, Rosa Parks and me. We were both born on February 4," Ruth said with a sense of pride, as she nodded and hummed softly to herself.

Burke smiled without explaining.

"I think that's part of why I always admired her, us sharing the same birthday and all. She was a little bit of a thing, but she wasn't afraid of anythin'. It was so much worse back then with all of those Jim Crow laws and people not being able to live together like God intended. Rosa stood up to that white bus driver and wouldn't give up her seat. No siree, no back of the bus for Rosa Parks."

Burke just nodded and hummed in agreement with his client as the patter of a soft summer rain began to tap against the window.

"Are there going to be any black people on our jury, Timmy?" she asked in a moment of uncertainty.

"I am sure there will be, Ruth. It's the law now. You can't prevent someone from sitting on a jury just because of their race."

"Are there...are there any black judges that might hear our case?"

"There are a few, but not many," he said, counting on the fingers of one hand.

"I mean, I don't want you getting the wrong idea, that I'm prejudiced or something, but it would be nice to have some black folks on the jury who knew what it was like being me."

"I will make sure there will be," Burke said, trying to reassure her.

"You know, I was always afraid of white folks, like they were better or smarter than me, but I see now that they're just people, full of the same fears and failures, just people like me. It was Rosa that gave me the courage to say the doctors were wrong about my Lonnie, that they should've done better by him."

"Well, I'm sure Rosa would be proud of you, Ruth, for not being afraid. I'm sure she would be happy just knowing she did something to help you to be brave."

"Funny, all this talk about birthdays, and I never even asked you when yours is. When is your birthday, Timmy?"

"February 4. Just like you, Ruth."

"Really, darlin'?"

"Really."

"Oh, Lordy. You and me and Rosa." Ruth smiled as the late-summer rain continued to fall.

THE DEPOSITION

A deposition is an opportunity for each side in a civil lawsuit to interview a party or witness on the other side of the case. The statement is taken under oath with a court reporter present to record the flow of questions and answers. Depositions are a great source of discovery and allow a lawyer to lock the deponent into his or her anticipated testimony at trial. It is also a chance to evaluate the person's ability to articulate his or her story.

The topics at a deposition are far-reaching, allowing considerable latitude into areas involving the plaintiff's background and basis for their lawsuit. Usually beginning with questions about the person's educational background and work history, the inquiry then shifts to the allegations in the complaint.

Ruth's deposition took place on a sunny day in August, 1990, at her lawyer's office. The parties had taken their seats, and after the witness was sworn, Charlie Dunn squirmed uncomfortably as he requested the plaintiff's date of birth.

"February 4, 1937." The frail woman smiled pleasantly and nodded knowingly to Burke.

Charlie Dunn was accustomed to winning the cases entrusted to his care by the largest and most prominent hospitals in the Boston area. He took no prisoners in the last legal blood sport called civil litigation. It frequently was anything but civil.

Sophisticated and with a broad knowledge of the medical profession, Sir Charles could change the course of a case with a single question that cast doubt about a party's credibility or motives. The deposition was just a preview of coming attractions at the trial.

"Can you tell us what problems your son Lonnie first exhibited which prompted you to seek out medical care for him?" Dunn began.

"He wasn't having a problem with illness. We had just moved and he was having problems in school adjusting to the new surroundings. He was having a reading problem. The school wanted to test him."

"Can you tell me where you moved from?"

"Yes, we moved out of Mattapan, in the city, because of the violence there. I wanted better for my children. I wanted Lonnie to grow up safe, so we moved to the suburbs. And the new school wanted to have him tested for learning disabilities. So I took him to see Dr. Rose at Massachusetts General Hospital," Ruth explained.

"I noticed that you are a single mother. What was the reason you parted company from your first husband?"

"He was abusive, and I was afraid for my life," Ruth said softly as her hands displayed a momentary tremor.

"He was physically abusive?"

"Yes, he was," she acknowledged without elaboration.

"Anyway, you said that you went to see Dr. Rose about your son. What did you relate to the doctor about Lonnie's reading problem?"

"We went over some forms, and the doctor asked if Lonnie was allergic to any medicines. I told him he was allergic to penicillin and was having headaches," Lonnie's mother explained.

"Did Dr. Rose prescribe anything on that date?"

"No, he put Lonnie on a reading program and told me to monitor his headaches over the next couple of months, and they set up an EEG. They did the EEG in August, and the doctor told me that they found a slight abnormality in the left-hand side of his head. I was upset, but the doctor told me, 'There's nothing to worry about. If there was anything seriously wrong with Lonnie, I would admit him into the hospital.' So I was a little relieved, and they set up another appointment to bring him in," Ruth said, her voice trailing off.

"Did you continue to monitor the headaches Lonnie was having between visits?"

"Yes, mostly in the morning, or late at night."

"What happened at the next visit?"

"It was September 15. We had some blood work done, and they set up a CT scan for November, and Dr. Rose gave us a prescription for the generic brand of Dilantin. I questioned him about the CT scan and what it was going to show."

As Ruth mentioned the prescription for Dilantin, Dunn unconsciously scribbled the word on a yellow legal pad, circling it three times with a number two pencil he used for taking notes.

"Dr. Rose said there was nothing seriously wrong with Lonnie and nothing for me to worry about, and I believed him. He gave me the prescription for three hundred milligrams of Dilantin and told me to give Lonnie one in the morning and two at night."

"Did you fill the prescription?"

"I went to the pharmacy to pick it up, and I asked the pharmacist what Dilantin was, and he told me it was used for seizures. I thought, well, maybe he's making a mistake, you know, because Lonnie doesn't have seizures, but he told me it was to prevent seizures too. So I started Lonnie on Dilantin that day, September 20," she said as tears welled in her eyes.

"Did he say anything about side effects?"

"No."

"Did you make a call to Dr. Rose to ask about the medicine?"

"No, not that first week."

There was an evenness to Ruth's responses. She needed no prompting. There was no doubt or hesitation as she explained the events leading to the loss of her Lonnie.

"Did you notice any changes in your son's condition after he was put on that medication?"

"Yes, I did. During that first week, Lonnie was just kinda slowing down. He was late in getting up in the morning. Before that he was always on time. Since the medicine, he was tired, just so tired. He wasn't having as many headaches, but he would come from school and lay down, go to bed, something he never did before."

"Did that bother you?"

"Yes, Lonnie was changing. He didn't have as much pep. He was falling asleep at school. The school nurse was calling. The teachers began to ask questions, you know, 'What's wrong with him?' So the next week I began to call Dr. Rose."

"What did he say when you called him?" There was a challenging tone to Dunn's voice as he raised his eyebrows skeptically.

"He would never say anything other than, 'If there was anything seriously wrong with Lonnie, I would admit him.' He never gave me an explanation of why he gave him the Dilantin. I called him quite often, whenever the school called me. Sometimes he would call me back, and sometimes he wouldn't. He would always say to make sure Lonnie was taking his medicine. 'Is he taking his medicine?' he'd ask. And I would say yes."

Ruth clasped the fingers of her right hand in a tight circle around her thin left wrist as she spoke. With each question she would twist and turn her wrist inside the same narrow space.

"Did Dr. Rose ever tell you that the medicine might make Lonnie drowsy?"

"No. I asked him, and he said no, it wasn't a side effect of the medicine. He never told me what the side effects were."

"Now, did something happen on October 7?"

"Yes, Lonnie went to football practice. He had made first-string running back. He was so proud. But the rule was that if he didn't go to school, he couldn't go to practice. That's my rule." Ruth nodded in agreement with herself.

"What happened at practice?" Dunn asked.

"About nine thirty, the coach brings him home from practice. The coach said Lonnie was lethargic today and blacked out on the field, and him and the other coach had to carry him off the field and put him on a cot. Lonnie told the coach, 'I was just tired today,' you know?"

"Is that all?"

"No, the coach said under no circumstances could he play or even practice football again without a doctor's letter. A couple of days later, I didn't have an appointment. It was October 10. I went into Dr. Rose's office."

"What did you say to him?"

"I have to calm down for a minute." Ruth hesitated as her eyes began to tear again.

She took a long breath, fought the emotion, and looked to Burke for support.

"Do you want to take a break, Ruth?"

"No, darlin', I'll be fine," she told her lawyer and began to speak again.

"When I came into his office that day, there were no people waiting. There was no secretary, and Dr. Rose wasn't in the office."

"Tell us what happened," Dunn coaxed softly.

The lawyers in the small conference room leaned forward as Ruth began.

"When Dr. Rose returned, I said, 'You didn't return my calls. The school has been calling me.' And I'm sitting here, he's at his desk, and Lonnie is behind him, and he just turns his back to me. He doesn't say anything to me and starts talking to Lonnie."

"What did he say?"

"Dr. Rose turned his back to me, and he says to Lonnie, 'How are you feeling, Lonnie?' And Lonnie says, 'Well, I feel all right, but my stomach has been bothering me.' Then the doctor says, 'How are the headaches?' And Lonnie tells him, 'I still have them off and on, but not as bad.' And he says, 'But my coach says I can't play football without a doctor's letter.'"

Charlie Dunn didn't interrupt the flow.

"That's all that was on Lonnie's mind. He just wanted a doctor's letter to play football. So I said, 'No, he can't play football. I need to know what's wrong with him.' I was worried. I was very upset."

"Yes," Dunn reluctantly agreed.

"He has Lonnie stand up, and he shines his little flashlight in Lonnie's eyes, and then he walks back to his desk and writes out the letter for him to play football. I told him I wanted another opinion. I said, 'Something is wrong with him. I want another doctor to see him. It's the medicine.' And he said, 'No, it's not the medicine.'"

"What did Dr. Rose do?"

"He says, 'Well, I'll set up an appointment with a pediatrician. His name is Dr. Kurtz. I'll call you later today and give you an appointment to see him.' Then he gave the letter to Lonnie and told him, 'Don't be worrying your mother.' He said, 'Just make sure you take your medicine. Are you taking it?' Lonnie smiled and told him, 'Yes, sir, I am taking it.' And then we left."

"How old was Lonnie at the time?"

"He was just thirteen," Lonnie's mother said as tears tracked both sides of her face.

"Did he have a rash at this time?"

"Yes, he did. It was a fine rash. It started like on the cheeks, around his nose." Ruth gestured to her own face as she spoke. "It was like a measles-type rash, you know what I mean?"

135

Dunn caught himself before he nodded in agreement and then leaned back.

"Did you see Dr. Kurtz?"

"The next day we did. Dr. Kurtz said Lonnie had strep and gave him a prescription for erythromycin, and I spoke to Dr. Rose, and he reduced the prescription for Dilantin to twice a day instead of three times."

"Did that help your son?"

"No, the next day Lonnie got worse. He was in constant pain and running a high fever. He wouldn't eat. I tried to bathe him to keep the fever down and gave him Tylenol. I called to try to get an ambulance to bring him to the hospital, but I didn't have insurance and the ambulance wouldn't come. The next day I took him back to see Dr. Kurtz at the hospital. It was October 13. We were late for the appointment. I don't have a car, and my friend was late to pick us up. I called to tell Dr. Kurtz, but he was aggravated. He said he couldn't see us because we were too late."

The tone had long since changed in Charlie Dunn's voice from skepticism to empathy. He didn't need to ask as Lonnie's mother explained her plight.

"I begged him. I told him Lonnie had been awful sick, and he was getting worse. He took him into his office to examine him. He came back out and told me to take him off the erythromycin because the tests came back and Lonnie didn't have any strep."

Dunn nodded as the woman continued.

"Dr. Kurtz seemed concerned and put Lonnie in a wheelchair because he couldn't walk and sent him downstairs to the emergency room. So I wheeled him down to the ER. We had to wait for several hours to be seen. The doctor there was very busy. They put Lonnie on a stretcher. He couldn't sit up. Finally, they took him in and did an examination and an x-ray. Then the ER doctor said he was sending Lonnie home because he couldn't find anything wrong with him. By then his temperature had gone down."

It seemed like Dunn wanted to say he was sorry as Ruth was speaking.

"I asked him to admit Lonnie, and he said no. I became frantic, and then the doctor just walked out. I got Lonnie dressed, and my ride had gone, so I took a cab from the hospital to my home that night."

"Did you tell the emergency room doctor that you thought the problem might be the Dilantin?"

"Yes, I did."

"Was he still taking the Dilantin?"

"No, I had just stopped it before that day. After that cab ride home, I started to take care of Lonnie myself. I didn't know what else to do. Then on October 16, I took him to the emergency room at Children's Hospital."

"How was your son's health during this time?"

"He was failing. His eyes had sunk back in his head. He lost so much weight. He wouldn't eat. I'd have to force him to drink fluids. His fever would elevate. I would sponge him with a towel to keep his fever down, just so he could sleep at night. He was like that every single night, until I took him to Children's late at night on the sixteenth."

"In your mind, he was getting worse?"

"Yes, he was. It was crowded when we got to the hospital. I brought a pillow and a blanket with us when I put him in the car. We had to help him out of the car. Lonnie couldn't sit up. They put him on a stretcher and brought him inside to the emergency room."

"What happened then?"

"The doctor that saw him that night was Dr. Rourke. He examined Lonnie and said to me right away, 'What kind of medicine has he been on?'"

"I told him, 'He was on Dilantin.'"

"He said, 'Is he still on it?'"

"I said, 'No, I stopped it a while back.'"

"Then he says, 'Thank God.' And then the doctor told me, 'Lonnie is in a drug fever caused by the Dilantin. The Dilantin is what's causing the rash.'"

Dunn nodded in agreement with Dr. Rourke's diagnosis as Ruth continued to speak.

"That was the first person that took the time to tell me what was going on with Lonnie, and I felt, 'Thank God, I finally got him somebody who is going to help him.'"

There was a fleeting sense of relief in the woman's voice as she relived the moment.

"What did Dr. Rourke do for you?"

"He said, 'Lonnie needs care right away. I am a research doctor. I don't usually work in the emergency room, but I am going to get you a doctor to help you out.' Then he went and brought back a woman doctor by the name of Willis."

"Tell us about that."

"Her and Dr. Rourke went out in the hallway to talk. I could hear them go back and forth, back and forth. Then Dr. Willis came back in and said they wanted to do some more tests, some blood work. Then she came back. It must have been around one in the morning, and she told me they weren't going to admit Lonnie because he told her he didn't want to stay."

"What did you say to Dr. Willis?"

"I told her it wasn't up to Lonnie. I said, 'He needs to be admitted.' Then Dr. Willis says, 'We're going to send him home tonight because we're not sure if he's in a drug fever. I want you to give him Tylenol, and I'll call you in the morning when the tests are in, and you can bring him back in then.' So I went home."

"Did you hear from Dr. Willis again?"

"Yes, the next morning she called and told me to bring him in and that they were going to admit him. Meanwhile, Dr. Kurtz called and wanted me to bring Lonnie in to see him at his office. I told him what had been going on and that they were going to admit him at Children's. That's what I did—I took him back to Children's Hospital."

"Tell us what happened when you brought him back the second time."

"They were waiting for him, and they did so many tests. We were there for all the day and half of the night. That's when Dr. Willis came out and told me that they weren't going to admit him because they thought he might have mono or hepatitis and that it could be treated at home. She wanted me to force fluids, give him Tylenol, watch him closely, and call her every day to see how he was doing. She said some of the test results weren't back yet and that her supervisor wasn't going to let her admit him. She made an appointment to see me on October 24. Then she sent me home again."

"Can you tell us what happened next in terms of your son's health?" Dunn asked quietly.

"Every day, he got worse and worse. The rash became like spider webs all over him. They were on his neck and the trunk of his body. His face was covered, down to his stomach. He was jaundiced. The bottom of his feet and his hands and fingernails were yellow. I would force fluids every hour, and as quick as I would put them in him he would lose them and vomit.

He would just lay in a deep sleep and moan. He would wake up scream-
ing, 'I'm hungry, I'm hungry, I want to eat.' I would bring him something,
and he wouldn't eat. His brothers and sisters all took turns making sure he
drank the fluids."

The questioning had essentially ceased as Ruth continued to speak
at will.

"Then on the twenty-third, Lonnie was in a fever all night, and he
would doze, and that's when I would rest, doze with him. Then he woke
up and began to scream, 'I can't see. Where is everybody? Where is everybody?' White mucus began to ooze from his body, from his rectum," Ruth
whispered as her own body began to shake and her hands clenched and
unclenched the lace handkerchief.

"Do you want to take a break, Ruth?" Burke asked, but she shook him
off and gently placed her hand on his.

"I'll be fine, darlin'," she told her lawyer.

"Did you tell Dr. Willis what was happening?"

"I called Dr. Willis every day, sometimes twice a day. Sometimes she
would call me back. She would tell me to give him the Tylenol and let her
know what was happening. That day I called her and told her I was bringing him in to the emergency room. It was a Sunday. All of his football
teammates and coaches were coming over to see him that day. They had
gifts for him, but Lonnie wasn't there because we had gone to the hospital.
When we got there they started an IV. He was so sick. Then Dr. Willis told
me again that they weren't going to admit him and that she was going to
send him back home."

"What did you do then, ma'am?" Dunn whispered as he carefully
placed the thin fingers of his right hand up to his forehead.

"I said, 'No, if I have to lay him on the floor in the emergency ward,
that's where we'll be, and the first thing in the morning, I'll leave and go
upstairs to the chief of staff. Somebody is going to admit my son. I am not
taking him back home.'"

"What did she say to that?"

"She came back in an hour or so with two other doctors, and they
admitted him to Division 86; it's a unit for the younger kids. They told me
he would be all right and I didn't have to stay. I could leave if I wanted to
and go home. So I did. I was dead tired on my feet. I hadn't slept in days."

"Did you return to the hospital?"

"Yes, the next day I went in to see him. They had put him in the back of the ward. You had to put on a gown and mask to go in and see him. The room was pitch-dark. He was put on an ice blanket, and they had a fan on him. He was allowed Jell-O and ice chips."

"Did you visit him daily?"

"Yes, every day. I would bring his brothers and sisters in to see him. I'd bathe him and feed him ice chips. They had this cream on the table next to his bed to apply to his face and his body. I would put that on him too."

"Did he appear to be getting any better?"

"He seemed the same, but he also seemed to perk up some, you know what I mean? Lonnie didn't want to be in the hospital. He didn't like the needles."

"Did something else happen to Lonnie while he was at Children's?"

"It was the morning. The last week of October. I called his room, and no one answered. So I got dressed and went in. When I got there, there was a roomful of doctors. The light was on, and Lonnie was laying flat on his bed. He had a heart-monitoring machine on him. Lonnie didn't respond to me when I walked in," Ruth explained as she bit down gently on her lower lip and slowly shook her head from side to side.

"I said to one of the doctors, 'What's going on? What's happening?'"

"One of the doctors said, 'During the night, Lonnie fell and hit his head. We're going to send him to the intensive care unit where he can be watched around the clock.' When they were moving him from his bed to a stretcher, I could see there was a suctioning machine attached to Lonnie. I could see blood in the suction machine."

The conference room went deadly still as Ruth struggled for her breath.

"Lonnie was in a coma for the next three days. I was with him every day. Then the last day he came out of it and screamed, 'Ma, Ma, where are you?' I was right there in his room, but he didn't realize it, you know what I mean?" Ruth said, looking for a moment of understanding as both men solemnly nodded.

"I would try to talk to Lonnie every day. Try to let him see me. Let him know I was there with him. Then on that last day, my Lonnie just slipped away. He died that day. The Good Lord took him," Ruth explained, grasping for the crucifix suspended from her neck for a small measure of comfort.

TARA

Boston in the eighties remained a city divided, writhing in the throes of court-ordered forced busing. The Federal Court's plan to integrate Boston's public schools had resulted in white flight from the inner city and black despair. For years, racial animosity and mistrust were the hallmarks of the chasm that separated entire communities.

Burke had grown up in a small town in upstate New York, cloistered and isolated in a world devoid of interaction with minorities of any form. He was the whitest of white bread, exposed to bigotry and racial intolerance on a daily basis, a life replete with blind hatred.

His experience as a prosecutor provided a limited introduction to other cultures, yet the reality remained—he had no black or Hispanic friends. Each meeting with Ruth became a form of indoctrination into a world Burke knew existed, but had experienced only from the periphery of his own life. It was the world divided by race. Two cultures separated by economic disparity and unequal opportunity.

The black woman and the white man sat talking in his office on the fourth floor of the North Market building. Outside, there was another soft summer rain falling, gently pelting against the partially opened windows of the conference room. Inside, Ruth opened another window into her day-to-day existence.

"I wanted my kids to have a better chance in life and to get a good education. That's why I moved out of Boston, to get away from all the hatred and violence. I didn't want them to learn to hate. There are times now when I lay awake at night and wonder if I made the right decision. I wonder if my Lonnie would still be alive today if I hadn't moved out of the city," Ruth said softly, her voice wavering.

"We can't go back, Ruth," Burke offered in a vain attempt to ease her pain.

There was a brief pause as she gathered her thoughts and steered the conversation in another direction.

Burke sensed there was something Ruth needed to explain that had somehow been left unsaid. There was an easy flow to the conversation as she translated her mental images into words.

"It seems like all my life I've never had anything that was really mine. I've always rented or had to live in subsidized housing. I was always living in somebody else's place. I never owned a house of my own. I always wanted a place where I could feel special just 'cause it was mine. A place for me and the rest of my kids. You know, the kinda place with a big front lawn."

Ruth closed her eyes as though she were picturing the scene of a warm August afternoon. In the background, the radio played a familiar song. The moment passed as reality returned and Ruth continued.

"Now every time I walk out the front door of my place at the Captain Cook project all I see is burnt-up grass, broken glass, and that darn television tower. It's so close it seems like it almost blocks out the sun. You can see it for miles around. Seems like it's right in my front yard. Do you have a lawn, Timmy?"

"Yeah, I do, Ruth."

"Good Lord, I never even owned a lawn mower, let alone mowed a lawn, but I like the idea. I love the smell of fresh cut grass. Sometimes I think of Lonnie and see him out front mowing this big green lawn that I never had," Ruth said as her voice drifted into an approving soft hum.

Burke listened without speaking, wondering why the two strangers from two very different places had been brought together.

"It's kinda strange, me being black and all, but one of my favorite movies is *Gone with the Wind.*"

"Really? Mine too."

"There's a scene in the movie when Scarlett's father tells her their plantation Tara is her roots. I always remembered that. I want to feel the same way someday. I want to have my own home. I want roots for my kids and me. Can you understand what I mean?"

Burke nodded slowly, recalling the scene from the movie.

"I don't want to feel guilty about our case, Timmy. This case has to mean something. I want it to mean that maybe Lonnie died to give his brothers and sisters a better chance in life. A chance to have a place of our own," she explained as her eyes filled with tears and slowly closed again.

Burke wished he could guarantee Ruth would have her own home with a big front yard, but the vast majority of medical malpractice claims resulted in verdicts in favor of the other side. He hesitated to tell her and squelch her dream of a new life. He suddenly felt it was a mistake to have taken the case, especially in an area of the law in which he had little practical experience.

He forced a wan smile that did little to hide his concern and his doubts.

"Don't worry, darlin'. I saw all those legal books you bought about medical malpractice cases. You did that for our case, didn't you?"

"Yes, I did," Burke told Ruth as she smiled and once again began to hum and nod in approval.

He was the lawyer, yet it was this frail woman who inspired him, confirmed his ability, eased his mind, and gave him courage to forge ahead.

Faith can do that to you.

"We're going to get you your own place, Ruth. You can call it Tara." He smiled as he spoke and then just as quickly regretted saying it.

LOST FAITH

Each time they met at his office, the black woman and white man spoke about their lives as well as the case. It was the first of November, 1990, the anniversary of Lonnie's death, and another of many meetings the two had in preparation for the upcoming trial, which had somehow become their trial. Ruth was an easy client in many ways. She readily accepted advice and direction about her pending testimony and what to expect from Charlie Dunn's cross-examination. Burke fluctuated between moments of confidence and abject fear that he would fail his client.

"You're still worried about losing our case, aren't you?" Ruth asked as she gathered her things to leave that afternoon.

"Yes, I am," Burke told her in a moment of weakness and honesty.

"Well, I just want you to know that I'm not afraid. I know God is with us."

"I wish I had your faith, Ruth, but I know how easy it is to lose a trial. A few years ago, I lost a big case when I was in the DA's office. It was a detective who was accused of stealing some money from a drug dealer. I felt like the whole world was counting on me. It was my first big trial, and when the jury came back with a 'not guilty,' I felt terrible and wouldn't talk to anyone for days. It was like I let everyone down because I failed."

"I'm sure you did your best, darlin'," Ruth tried to reassure him. "Sometimes it's more about the trying than the winning."

"It was a difficult time for me personally," Burke began and then paused, afraid to express his inner thoughts.

"It's OK, you can tell me," Ruth's voice coaxed.

145

"It's just that right after that trial ended one of my brothers died of a heart attack. He was only thirty-five with two little boys. I was there with him at the end, holding his hand when he died."

There was an unspoken connection as Ruth visualized a similar moment holding Lonnie's hand at the time of his death.

"A few months later, my father fell from a ladder and died. My wife was pregnant with twins at the same time, and we lost them both shortly after that...it was a bad year."

Burke cleared his throat before he continued.

"I think...I think that's when I stopped believing."

The woman said nothing and reached across the oak table, softly placing the hollow of her hand atop her lawyer's.

REFLECTIONS

The framed mirror behind the mahogany bar at Crickets reflected Burke's upper body as he sat alone nursing his Tanqueray and tonic with two slices of lime. The soft glow of the white decorator lights wrapped around the trees warmed the interior of the bar from the darkness of early November.

Somehow the lights made it feel more like Christmas.

Outside, the traffic was backed up on the ramp outside Faneuil Hall. Above the Dockside Garage, a string of slow-moving white headlights and red taillights decorated both sides of Route 93, all the way from Charlestown to Dorchester.

It had become a routine on Fridays after work to visit the local watering hole where other lawyers gathered to exchange war stories from the past week. Burke was well into his first drink, at the point where the buzz had slowly begun to ease his mind.

Ruth's trial was less than two months away.

The bar was crowded with three-piece suits jockeying for recognition, but you could still hear Sade singing "Smooth Operator" on the speaker overhead.

Burke didn't initially see the man as he edged toward the straight-backed stool next to his. Dressed in a conservative dark blue suit, the man had graying hair, a thin build, and fine-boned hands. When the stranger spoke, Burke recognized the now-familiar voice. He had recently spent three hours listening to the man in the dark blue suit question his client.

It was Charlie Dunn.

"Hey, Counselor, can I buy you a drink?" Sir Charles offered.

There was a momentary hesitation that quickly evaporated as his opponent extended his right hand.

"Sure, thanks, Mr., ah, Charlie," Burke corrected himself. He smiled broadly and reached back for Dunn's hand as the older man eased his lanky frame onto a nearby stool.

Over the next half hour, the two men shared a drink and compared notes on the law, their families, the Red Sox, Boston traffic, politics, the weather—just about everything except their mutual case. The noise from the bar gradually eased as the crowd thinned into the chilly night air.

The pair sat alone at the end of the bar as Charlie Dunn spoke about his life, a topic eased open by the effects of the alcohol and the need to be understood. Burke listened intently to his adversary, wondering how relative strangers can share their innermost thoughts.

"I seldom talk about it much now, but I lost my first wife to a brain tumor. She died right after I began practicing law. We had the whole world ahead of us. We made so many plans. She was only twenty-nine," Dunn explained in a moment of candor as the waiter brought another round.

"I'm so sorry, Charlie," Burke said in a muffled voice as he thought of the uncertainty of life and his own loss of faith.

"Guess I was just angry at the world after that. I loved her so much. I quit the law. I started drinking, chasing women, just trying to find someone to love. I fell into this dark, deep hole, and then one day I snapped out of it. I learned you can't wish away your sorrows. It was all a bad dream until I met my current wife, Janice. She got me back on track, got me to devote myself to my work, the law. I don't know where I'd be now if it wasn't for her."

There was a moment of sadness that settled around the lawyer for Children's Hospital as he looked downward, pausing to shake the ice in his drink.

"I think everything happens for a reason, Charlie. Nothing is random, we just don't know why," Burke said, sounding very much like Ruth.

"Maybe, maybe you're right." Dunn nodded in response without lifting his head.

Outside the bar, the traffic had eased on the Southeast Expressway as the season's first snowfall slowly changed the city's palette from a dense gray to varying shades of drifting white. Burke saw his image reflected in the mirror above the bar and realized it was time to go. The two men shook hands, wished each other well in their upcoming trial, and headed their separate ways.

Burke walked back to his office, turned on the green-shaded library light on the corner of his desk, and sat quietly listening to the music of the night.

He began to think about his life, his connection to Holly, Deirdre, Ruth, and Charlie Dunn, and for some reason he began to cry.

THE CARETAKER

Shirley McConnell was the only child of a seamstress and a house painter. She had grown up in a poor, black section of Dorchester in a time of racial turmoil for a city divided. Her father, she was proud to say, was a jack-of-all-trades who helped build the Callahan Tunnel. Uninspired in high school, she left in the tenth grade, and despite the lack of a GED, she worked for various local businesses until the drugs took her.

It had been more than three years since the murder of Sherman Griffiths when McConnell, clean and sober for a year, was interviewed in Burke's office. Frank Lynch, the attorney for the Bellevue Street landlords, took his seat and smiled apprehensively at the quiet black woman seated opposite him.

Shirley's deposition was like so many others—with a stenographer, the witness, and the attorneys from the two different camps huddled around a conference table, anxiously bleeding information from the nervous witness. Newman had located the former resident of Bellevue Street living on another dangerous Dorchester street, this time freed of her addiction. Surprisingly, Shirley offered to help the officer's widow and tell what she knew about the Jamaicans. She told Deirdre's lawyers it had something to do with redemption.

"Can you tell us what you know about Bellevue Street?" Newman began as the stenographer dutifully took the exact measure of her words.

"I moved there with my daughter and my husband. He was working at the Hotel Milner for about six months at the time. When we first moved in, there was a person named Star living on the third floor. He was a Jamaican, early thirties, short, with dark skin. Then a guy named Roddy moved in. He was in his late twenties. Then another guy with a scar on his face moved in. Then there was Arthur. His real name was Albert Lewin. They were all Jamaicans."

"How did you get to know this Arthur, Albert Lewin?"

"From buying drugs. I had been buying from the previous occupants before him, Star and Roddy. Then Albert got there a couple of months before the shooting," Shirley said without hesitation.

There was an easy flow to her speech. Each question was followed by a quick response, without veneer or affect. It was an honest portrayal of an addict's life as she lived it, without denial or rationalization.

"Can you just kind of lay it out for us how that worked?"

"Yes. At first, they would never open up the front door. After a while I started to use the back stairs after I got to know them. They had been robbed a few times. So they stopped opening the front door, and the money would go through the little like peephole and drugs out. When I first moved in there was an entirely different door there, but they got robbed so many times they put the steel door up with the bars behind it. They had a different door before Albert got there."

"How did you know these guys had gotten robbed before?"

"One of the Jamaican guys came down and told me. There was no phone on the third floor, so I used to pass messages to this guy by the name of Smudge who was the main man, another Jamaican. I told Smudge that there had been another robbery, that they had broke in, and he told me to go upstairs where the stash was and get the stuff. So I did. I removed the drugs and brought them down to my apartment. It was about a month before the shooting took place. I took out a gun and some coke. They kept 'em in a bag of rice."

"How bad were you using during this period, Shirley?" Newman asked, tentatively; perhaps fearful of her answer.

"At the time, I was a drug addict, using cocaine. I freebased it, sometimes every day, just smoking it through a pipe or a Pepsi bottle. It's expensive, you know. Sometimes I would go without using it. Some others, I would smoke all day long. People would come to me, people that I knew, and ask me to go upstairs and buy for them. I would get a piece of whatever they bought."

Each answer brought another, and with it a better understanding of Shirley's gradual descent into a life devoid of meaning. An existence wrapped around a coke spoon, a cloud of mind-numbing deadness that coursed through the blood of her veins at a hundred and six miles an hour.

"How much were they selling?"

"Usually they sold forties and eighties, two different sizes, forty bucks and eighty bucks. Sometimes I would wash clothes for the guys upstairs, clean their apartment. They didn't have any heat on the third floor, no hot water. So sometimes they would use my shower, in my apartment, and pay me in cocaine. They usually just sold cocaine, but they had herb there too. The Jamaicans smoked their coke in with the herb, mixed it, that's how they did theirs."

"What else can you tell us about the Jamaicans?" Newman asked as Lynch shifted uncomfortably in his chair.

"They ate out all the time. They didn't cook. They loved fast food. My husband, Jimmy, used to go to the store for them to get goat meat and rice."

"Were there many people coming in and out of the place?"

"Yes, see everybody I knew was a drug user, and they all came to Bellevue Street, sometimes every day. After I would buy it for my friends, I would bring it back downstairs and cook it for them with baking soda in a glass tube. I'd put it on a fire and cook it until it became like a rock. It don't have the chemicals in it that crack does."

With each question asked, the stenographer leaned into Shirley's answer, at times wide-eyed to a side of life previously unseen.

"Was it like this every day?"

"Yes, sometimes the hallway got too crowded. My husband Jimmy was like a bouncer. He used to watch out for them upstairs. Run errands, like go to the liquor store for them. There was a lot of traffic, a lot of males in the building. Jimmy looked tougher than me. Somebody had to be in control to keep traffic out of the hallway. There was never much noise because Jimmy kept things to a minimum. You basically couldn't control the drug traffic coming in, but once business was done you had to leave. Twenty-four hours a day, seven days a week, holidays too, usually more at night. People would sleep during the day but be up until two in the morning. It was no suits and ties, just street people."

"How often did you see Albert?"

"I saw Albert a lot toward the end. I saw him with a gun a couple of times, before they changed the door. He used to open the old door with a gun in his hand. One time he threatened me with it because he owed me something and he didn't want to pay me. This was before I got to know him good, like two months before the shooting. He tolerated me, but none of us actually liked each other."

As he listened to Shirley's story about Bellevue Street, Newman knew the quiet woman would be a key to any possible success in Deirdre's case. The case rose or fell on their ability to show what the landlord knew, or should have known, about his property.

"How about Mr. Campbell, the new owner of the building. Can you tell us about him?"

"I met Mr. Campbell when they took over the building. He asked me to take care of the building. I was the caretaker. I swept up, picked up the trash. I told him I used to do it for the previous owner, and he asked me to continue doing it."

"Was Mr. Campbell ever on the premises during the time of this heavy foot traffic?"

"Yes, but there wasn't any drugs apparent, but they were present. People used to bag their drugs in lottery slips and little corners of plastic bags. There were lots of them around the property. It was folded up into a little packet with a tight little paper seal with the cocaine inside. It should've been obvious drugs were being sold, just from the amount of traffic of street people coming in and out of the building."

"What do you remember about the day of the shooting?" Newman asked, shifting the focus of his inquiry.

"I remember hearing the gunfire from the hallway. I was in my kitchen. I didn't know the police were even there when it happened. I was freebasing when I heard the gunshots, so I started to clean off my kitchen table, putting everything away. I went to the front door of my apartment and then came back to my kitchen. That's when Albert was at the back door. I don't lock the backdoor—that's how Albert got in. I remember he had a fur-lined jacket on."

Newman nodded and waited for Shirley to continue.

"Albert was like natural, not rushing or anything. Albert just sat down with everyone else. He had the gun and the drugs. He had money and handed it to me. I didn't learn what happened to the gun until later on. The police said they found the gun underneath the mattress in the bedroom, my mattress. Albert told me someone was trying to break in upstairs, like

154

it was just another rip-off," Shirley told the attorneys, mimicking Lewin's nonchalance.

"What happened next?"

"After this, I went to the front door, and the police officer outside told me to close it. I still didn't know what had happened upstairs. I just thought someone had called the police because of the gunfire. The police were talking to the girl in the apartment across the hall. I heard her tell them that he, the guy from the third floor, would be in my apartment, that Albert would be in there, and that's when I opened the door and let the police in," Shirley explained.

"What happened after they came inside your apartment?" Newman asked.

"When the police came in, I didn't say anything right there because the Jamaican posse aren't people you want to get involved in with as far as giving up information to the police. So I talked to the police in the kitchen. The Jamaicans were new, back then, you know, they were rough people. I was involved in drugs, but I never did nothing as far as people's lives." The woman shook her head and for the first time bit down on her front lip.

"I understand," Newman offered.

"I think that's when I found out that an officer been shot upstairs. I told them I know that Albert is the only one that came downstairs. I'm not saying he was the only one up there, but..."

"Is that what you told them?"

"Yes, and like anytime people are in trouble and they do wrong, they never tell the full truth, they always tell half truths, like it was a little bit of truth here, and a little bit of lies there. Because you don't want to admit you were sitting there getting high. You don't want to admit to doing certain things. You want to get the truth across, but you're still trying to cover yourself."

"This guy Smudge, is there anything else that you remember about him?"

"Yeah, Smudge came there twice a week, sometimes with his wife. He was the headman, the head honcho. He was the one at the top, the one that supplied the cocaine. He was the one that everyone worked for. Smudge was really Delray Ferguson. He's the one told me where the stash was in the bag of rice. Smudge gave everybody a new rented car too."

"Did you ever see Smudge talk to any of the owners of the building?"

"Yeah, I saw Mr. Campbell talking to Smudge a couple of times outside in front of the house. I assumed he knew what was going on. I assumed the police knew, too. The whole neighborhood knew. The place never closed down. Every three or four months somebody new was living in that third-floor apartment. The conditions were lousy. It was half furnished; nobody tried to fix it up. No heat, no lights, no hot water. You'd have to be blind and deaf not to know. *Everybody* knew that drugs were being sold there," the caretaker explained in sync with the silent rhythm of the stenographer's keystrokes.

PURPLE MARTINS

The call from the lawyer for Children's Hospital came early on a dreary Tuesday morning in late January 1991.

It was a raw day, with an unrelenting wind that drove the rain and sleet sideways amid an array of multicolored rain slickers, mangled umbrellas, slashing windshield wipers, and useless, soggy *Globes* and *Heralds* held aloft for protection from the downpour.

Charlie Dunn was on the line with a note of acceptance in his voice. The two lawyers had come to respect each other despite the adversarial nature of their relationship. It had been over four years since they first met at the tribunal hearing in courtroom 313. Burke had learned a great deal about the attorney on the other side of Ruth's case during that time. The call wasn't what he had come to expect.

"I want to talk to you about your case...," Sir Charles opened and paused, midsentence, recalling a moment in his own life.

He wasn't particularly religious, but Dunn pictured himself alone, like Lonnie, in a hospital bed many years before. Riddled with tuberculosis, frightened and weak, struggling to breathe, the lawyer for Children's at that moment wondered why God had chosen to spare him then and years later decided to take Ruth's child.

Dunn quickly put the thought aside. He feigned a half cough, then made an apology and forged ahead with the request to discuss the case.

"Sure. What do you want to talk about?" Burke responded evenly.

"Your lady has made quite an impression on me."

"She's been through hell, Charlie. Losing a child..."

"Yeah, she has. We both know a little bit about loss," Dunn said without elaboration.

157

When the telephone conversation was concluded, Burke hung up and immediately called Ruth. Despite the storm, she was in his office within the hour, delivered safely by a big yellow taxi. She wore a clear plastic bonnet over her curls and the same print flowered dress she'd had on the first day her lawyer had met her. Even though it was raining and cold, she was smiling.

Ruth took her customary seat in the glassed-in conference room, surveyed the space, as was her practice, and turned her head to speak without moving her body.

"Did I ever tell you about my favorite birds?" Ruth asked before Burke could tell her the news.

"No, I don't think you ever did."

"They're purple martins. They're these little birds that travel all the way from Brazil to Boston. They migrate here from the Amazon River. They fly thousands of miles to get here. They're the kind of birds that love to be around people, but they don't build their own nests. They need to have someone, people, do it for them."

"OK," the lawyer agreed without knowing why.

"And these purple martins give people their song in return. I was thinking on my way here today that you've made me feel like one of those little birds. Like I've been on this long journey and you're trying so hard to build a place for me to live, but I feel bad because I don't know how to sing." His client smiled.

Burke wanted to tell Ruth she had already given him her song, her message of life, but he was uncertain, afraid to show any emotion.

"Lordy, listen to me just carrying on like this. You sounded so excited when you called. What did you want to tell me?" she asked, breaking the silence.

"I just got a call from Mr. Dunn. He told me they want to settle your case. There isn't going to be a trial. You're going to be able to get your house...your own Tara," Burke told Ruth as she instinctively reached for her crucifix and began to cry.

THE WILL

The resolution of Ruth's case seemed to add more hours to each workday. Burke missed his frequent contact with the new owner of a red brick home with its large green front lawn. It made him feel a shared sense of pride whenever Ruth would refer to the new home as "her Tara." Despite her absence from his life, he thought of Ruth often.

There were times when he picked up the receiver to call, but he never did, still afraid to show any emotion. Besides, it seemed there were always other pressing matters to contend with.

The two lawyers at Faneuil Hall had long since committed themselves to resolving the chaotic aftermath of the murder at Bellevue Street. Their case was neatly catalogued as a civil lawsuit, but its significance felt more like a criminal prosecution. The ingredients were all there: a killer gone free, the unseen drug underworld, media criticisms of police failures, and worse, the false affidavit submitted by Carlos Luna.

Through it all, the two men had grown attached to Sherm's widow. She, like Ruth, was an easy client to deal with. There was no drama, no demands, just a simple request for the two men to help sort out the meaning of her loss.

She could have cried, but she never did. She could have chosen to complain about her life or the unfairness of being widowed with two young girls, but she chose not to. She would have been warranted to embrace bitterness, even rage, for the mistakes made by the other members of the drug unit, but she never did.

"I just need to know the truth. I want to know why Sherm died. Whatever it is. I can live with the truth," Deirdre told the pair.

Failure was not an option.

Like any major litigation, Deirdre's case was a constant influx of paperwork, discovery of witnesses, and the marshaling of information. Months, even years of preparation led to a short-lived trial, frequently lasting only a few days. Along with Shirley McConnell, the two Faneuil Hall lawyers had recently located another witness willing to testify about the Jamaicans at Bellevue Street.

He was a drug dealer whose name was Rodney Black.

*****

A telephone call came in the midst of another day of discovery in Deirdre's case.

"There's a call I think you should take, Tim," the office administrator explained as Burke stared at the flashing amber light on his phone and reached for the handset.

"Hello."

"How's my favorite lawyer?" the familiar woman's voice on the telephone asked.

"Great, Ruth, how's my favorite client?"

"Oh, I'm doing all right I guess," she said with a note of uncertainty.

It had been months since the pair had spoken, yet the connection, the history of emotion was still present. The lawyer unexpectedly realized how much he missed the feeling that she was ever-present in his life.

"I need you to do something for me, darlin'."

"Sure, whatever you need, Ruth," Burke told her.

"I want to set up a time to have you do up my will."

"OK," he told her as a sense of fear and a sudden shudder of loss ran through his body.

In that instant Burke knew Ruth was dying.

The heart that held so much love was failing…it was simply a matter of time.

No longer afraid to show emotion, he made the trip to the hospital twice that week to check on her. Both times she was asleep in her bed, breathing deeply with a smile of serenity possessed only by those with a clear conscience. Ruth's bare arms were draped on each side of her thin body, with the rest of her wrapped in white linens. The contrast highlighted her skin, making it appear darker than it was. Her eyes remained closed while Burke stood quietly studying the older woman's face.

He briefly thought of the night Lonnie died and the pain of Ruth's life as she had prayed for God to take her instead of her son. Burke quietly took three strides forward, carefully placed the bouquet of daffodils near the nightstand, and turned to leave.

As he reached for the door, there was a stir behind him.

"Hello, darlin'. Did you remember to bring the papers for my will?" Ruth asked in a voice barely above a church whisper.

"I did, Ruth, but you won't need to worry about your will for a long time from now," Burke lied as he turned back to stand next to the side of her bed.

She smiled a faint smile as he took her hand.

"Darlin', I 'preciate you trying to make me feel good, but you and I both know the Good Lord's told me to pack my bags. I'm not afraid to leave this earth. I'm happy 'cause I'm going to get to see my Lonnie again. It's been so many years since I held him that night in the hospital. Do you think he's gotten any taller?"

"I don't know if people continue to grow after they die, Ruth."

"I think you've grown since I first met you that day in your office. Your heart's bigger now. I think that's why God brought us together. He wanted me to teach you about His gift of faith," the dying woman explained.

"What do you mean?" the lawyer asked.

What Ruth told him would stay etched in his mind for the remainder of his life.

COURTROOM 10

Located at the intersection of Court and High Streets in the shire town of Dedham, Massachusetts, the landmark Greek Revival style courthouse first opened its doors to the halls of justice in 1827.

Tucked neatly into the southwest corner of the granite block building, courtroom 10 was a smaller version of the primary courtroom one flight above. The double-door entrance to the courtroom was encased with fifteen-foot, faded wood trim and frosted panes of translucent glass scripted with the words "Supreme Court." The heavy doorknob was timeworn to a partial brassy sheen that, if you looked carefully, revealed the words "The County of Norfolk, 1793" imprinted in a circle around the handle's facing.

Nearby, two uncomfortable maple benches provided limited reason to linger outside the courtroom.

Across the hall from courtroom 10 was the office of the clerk of courts, Walter F. Timilty, an earnest and youthful-appearing attorney responsible for the day-to-day flow of cases passing through the court system. Outside the door to the clerk's office, two ornate wood-and-glass pay telephone booths sat idle for the majority of the day, and when opened, they revealed the faint scent of cheap wood pulp and ink from years of Yellow Pages stored within. For some undisclosed reason, a foot-square mahogany mailbox with a neatly written sign that read, "Do not post mail here," separated the two cubicles.

The outer lobby separating the two rooms was a sparse setting of mottled gray marble floors and walls decorated by equally Spartan collections of photographs of past members of the local county bar association. Without apparent reason, the random years of 1949 and 1967 were prominently featured in a historical tribute to the attorneys who'd spent their time and efforts within courtroom 10.

It was the Friday before Labor Day weekend as the two lawyers for the plaintiff stood outside courtroom 10 waiting for their case to be called. The hearing that day was a brief appearance to determine the assignment of the trial judge and to argue any last-minute motions before the start of the Griffiths trial following the holiday weekend.

"Did you know that in 1949 there were only six women attorneys in Norfolk County and about a hundred and forty guys?" Burke mentioned after counting the rows of photographs depicted within the picture frame.

"I'm not surprised," Newman responded.

"It didn't get a whole lot better by 1967 either."

"How many?"

"Hang on a second. About, let's see, three hundred and ninety men and nine women," Burke said after doing the math.

"You're kidding, right?"

"No, take a look," Burke said, gesturing to the stark black-and-white photographs staring back from behind the glass.

"It's incredible to think of the way it was back then and how things have changed. Did you find out who is going to be sitting on our case yet?"

"Yeah, I did. I just checked with the clerk's office. It's Judge Elizabeth Butler. They said she used to do insurance defense work before she became a judge."

"I'm sure she'll be fine," Newman allowed as the pair turned toward the double doors. "You want to go inside and wait?"

The interior of courtroom 10 was a throwback to a bygone era of nineteenth-century architecture. Faded wainscoting continued from the wood-framed public entrance to the opposite side of the courtroom leading to the judge's chambers. Time had stood still since the room's construction, witnessed by the stoppage of the pendulum of an ancient timepiece suspended above the judge's leather chair. The decorative tongue-and-dot wood trim, dental moldings, and delicate carvings resembling pineapples added an aura of Colonial hospitality to an otherwise intimidating scene.

The room itself was a large open space with high ceilings, suspended half-moon lights, and three broad windows embedded within each of the three walls surrounding the elevated bench. The windows were separated into sixteen rectangular panes of glass that provided a panoramic view of the freshly mowed lawn leading out to Court and High Streets. Each of the streets was sprinkled with measured rows of magnificent maples and stately Victorian homes guarded by whitewashed wooden fences.

For some unknown reason, the scene reminded Burke of Hannibal, Missouri, Tom Sawyer, and the trial of Injun' Joe.

JUDGE BUTLER

A graduate of Smith College, Elizabeth "Beth" Butler began her legal career at Boston College Law School. After a brief two-year stint in the Middlesex DA's office, she moved into the private sector, eventually spending over seven years at the law firm of Morrison, Mahoney & Miller.

The 3 Ms sounded like a trio of Irishmen just off the boat from the old sod, but it was the go-to firm for the insurance industry's defense of literally thousands of claims brought each year by plaintiffs in every imaginable type of personal injury lawsuit. From rear-end car accidents to train wrecks, from medical malpractice to dramshop claims, the law firm was a proving ground for lawyers looking for variety in their caseload. Eschewing plaintiff's work, their office frequently provided the defense for premises liability cases like Deirdre's.

Butler rose quickly within the firm, making partner along the way, despite the inherent bias against women in the legal profession. Highly regarded by her peers, she was sought out for a judgeship and readily accepted. Blonde and younger that most of her judicial contemporaries, Butler's caseload ranged from murder cases to esoteric civil litigation. She had this quirk about not allowing the lawyers to refer to a witness by his or her first name during direct or cross-examination, maintaining the decorum and the dignity of the court.

In Burke's experience, even when she ruled against him, there was an easy grace about her, a style in her decision making that made him feel he was treated fairly.

Her Honor greeted the lawyers for both sides warmly that afternoon in courtroom 10. The four attorneys formally introduced themselves from their respective locations, plaintiff's table in front, and defense directly behind, both adjoining the jurors' box to their right.

"Good afternoon, Your Honor," Frank Lynch began, identifying himself and co-counsel, William Smith, from the law firm of Lecomte, Emanuelson, Tick & Doyle.

Lynch, like Judge Butler and Newman, was a graduate of Boston College Law School. He was a skilled attorney who saw Deirdre's case as one of the most significant challenges of his legal career. He had become a familiar face as a result of the hours spent on the opposite side of a conference table, taking the depositions of the witnesses and parties to the case.

Retained by Preferred Mutual, a large insurance company that provided coverage for the building on 102–104 Bellevue Street, the defense attorney had spent parts of the past several years preparing for the trial that would last less than a week. A fair guy, without guile, Lynch's view of the evidence was diametrically opposed to the viewpoint of Deirdre's two lawyers. It was clear that there would be no last-minute offer of settlement.

"I guess that's why we have trials," Burke told his adversary at the end of their brief session before Judge Butler.

The four men shook hands in the lobby, sandwiched between the framed collections of photographs of attorneys from days gone by. Like the attorneys featured in the composites hanging on the walls, courtroom 10 would provide the battleground to test their legal positions. The lawyers wished each other luck without enthusiasm and headed in different directions. Jury selection would start first thing following the Labor Day weekend.

The following Tuesday came quickly.

It was a pleasant day, with the warmth of summer still in the September air. There was a level of distraction from an unexpected pennant run by the Red Sox. The team had left behind a woeful spell of disappointing mediocrity to lead their division as summer waned. The chance of a World Series visit was a clear possibility.

The lawyers settled into their seats with their boxes of evidence, reams of documents, legal pads, and trial notebooks scattered across the narrow expanse of both counsel tables. Her Honor took her seat, introduced the names of the parties involved, and asked the one hundred faces staring back at her about their potential connection or bias in the case.

The jury selection process was a familiar experience. Each side had about a minute to review the name, age, occupation of each candidate and their spouse, their education, criminal history, prior jury experience, number of children, their personal bias about serving, and life in general.

At the end of Judge Butler's address, the jurors were asked to bring their issues to the attention of a court officer who would, in turn, bring the potential juror forward to the sidebar to speak to counsel and Her Honor.

Eager to please, and dressed appropriately for the occasion, the middle-aged Hispanic woman anxiously approached the judge's bench with her juror card held aloft like a Roman shield. She was the next person in line to be seated on the jury deciding the fate of Deirdre's case.

"Yes, ma'am, you raised your hand with a question," Her Honor said with a smile. "Is there something that you want to share with us?"

"Yes, yes. You asked if any of us knew anyone associated with the case, whether we knew any of the people that were involved."

There were the usual wing nuts who wanted no part of sitting on a jury, using any excuse to avoid a commitment to their civic duty. Neither of the lawyers, plaintiff nor defense, wanted any part of them deciding a case of this importance. This woman was different. She was educated, sincere, and obviously well intentioned.

"Yes, who is it?"

"I just wanted to tell you that my husband is Carlos Luna. He was a police officer in the drug unit with the Boston police that night. I don't think I can be impartial," Mrs. Luna explained.

There was a four-second delay before the judge or any of the lawyers spoke.

"I just want to thank you, Mrs. Luna, for bringing that to our attention. That was the right thing to do. We appreciate your willingness to serve. You may return to the jury pool to possibly sit on another case, but we won't be able to have you serve on this jury."

Burke looked at Newman and wanted to say something about strange coincidences, but he wasn't able to fit the words into a meaningful sentence.

THE FIRST WITNESS

Jury selection and both opening statements were completed quickly. The trial was about to begin.

There was a feeling of hesitant anticipation in the courtroom as Burke took his customary position at the far end of the jury enclosure. The lawyer loved and simultaneously dreaded this very moment, feeling it akin to being strapped into the front-row death seat of an undulating, high-rise roller coaster. He glanced apprehensively at the unknown faces of the recently chosen jurors and quickly turned toward the white-shirted court officer.

"Brendan Bradley, please," he said, swallowing hard.

The request was made to the bailiff, who quickly left the courtroom, exiting through the double swinging glass-paned doors to retrieve the first witness in the plaintiff's case.

The man walked at an easy pace across the width of the courtroom, past the fixed scrutiny of the fourteen jurors. He was a grizzled sort, with blue eyes, a long jawline, bushy eyebrows, and a slumping posture that underscored the weight of his years of detective work. A Boston cop for nearly three decades, he rose to the rank of captain and spent seven years in the homicide unit.

Brendan Bradley had grown up in Savin Hill, an Irish enclave of Dorchester, six minutes from Bellevue Street. He was the firstborn son of a woman from County Cork who made the long journey to Boston during the Great Depression. A person of faith, she left her home and family in Ireland as a teenager, traveling alone across the stormy Atlantic in search of a better life. It was a little thing, but each day Bradley thought of his mother's courage.

How proud you make me feel, bein' an officer of the law and all, Bradley could hear her say as he strode to the witness enclosure.

"Would you face me and raise your right hand," Clerk Walter Timilty formally said as the woman in the black robe looked on.

Once the oath was taken, the questioning began. There was a feeling of comfortable familiarity to the Q and A between the former detective and the attorney. The witness stated his complete name, spelled the second half of it for the benefit of the court reporter, and then turned to the gallery to see if Deirdre was present.

Bradley felt a sense of personal failure for the acquittal of Albert Lewin. He came upon the frenzied chaos at Bellevue Street an hour after the shots had been fired. By that time, the integrity of the crime scene was irretrievably lost. He took possession of three .45-caliber shell casings found just inside the doorsill to the third-floor apartment before obtaining a search warrant. Bradley believed them to be covered by an exception to the requirement of a search warrant that allows the seizure of evidence in "plain view."

The Massachusetts Supreme Judicial Court ruled otherwise, suppressing the shell casings and the admissibility of the steel door seized from inside the apartment.

"Have you ever had occasion to investigate any homicide cases?" Burke began the introduction.

"Yes, sir, approximately a hundred and thirty of them," the witness answered without fanfare.

"Did you investigate the homicide of Sherman Griffiths?"

"Yes, I did. I got a call and responded to 102–104 Bellevue Street, in the Dorchester section of Boston."

"Can you tell the jury what you saw when you arrived there?" Burke asked, settling into the all-too-familiar role of explaining crime scenes to a rapt audience of twelve jurors and two alternates.

It was clear the jurors were in the process of sizing up the first witness for the plaintiff, shifting forward to hear every word.

"It was mass confusion," Bradley began. "I had to park two blocks away. I was informed that a police officer had been shot while executing a search warrant for drugs on the third-floor landing."

"What did you observe when you went there?"

The questions were a building-block presentation of evidence, taking the jurors through the drama as viewed by an on-scene witness.

"There was no door on the 104 side of the building. It had been taken right off of the hinges. There was blood on the landing. There was a base-ball hat identified as belonging to Sherman Griffiths, a pair of glasses, and some empty shell casings just inside the threshold of the apartment."

At the mention of Sherm's hat and the blood on the landing, Bradley glanced toward the gallery to assess Deirdre's reaction. He momentarily felt the need to apologize again, to explain, but there was no time.

"Can you describe the door for us?"

"It was a grayish-bluish steel-type door that had a hole in it and a peep-hole also."

"Have you ever seen that type of door before with a peephole *and* another hole underneath it?"

"Not that I can ever recall," Bradley stated as he shook his head.

"Were you able to determine the caliber of those shell casings later?"

"Yes, they were .45-calibers."

"Were you able to determine what caliber bullet was used in the shoot-ing death of Sherman Griffiths?"

"Objection," Lynch blurted.

"Sustained," Her Honor quickly added with a nearly imperceptive shake of her head.

Burke knew better than to press the matter.

"Can you describe the interior of the apartment on the third floor?"

"It was sparsely furnished. Not in very good condition, I would say."

There were numerous eight-by-eleven-inch pictures providing gritty glimpses of the scene captured after the fact. The lawyer took the entire stack from the plaintiff's table and approached the witness stand.

"I show you these photographs of the interior of that apartment and ask you if they accurately depict the appearance of the apartment that evening?"

It was the first opportunity for the jury to see the murder scene as Bradley explained what they were observing. There was a somber starkness to the moment, not just in the photographs, but also in the reality of life, the sense of loss and the suddenness of death.

"Yes, they do. These are some snow tires on the left where you enter, and this is the intercom system on the wall."

"Can you tell the jury what these are photographs of?" Burke asked as he held another exhibit aloft for the jury to see.

"These are photographs of a pair of two-by-fours that were held in place by metal brackets type thing. When I got there the door was off its hinges, so I had it put back in place to show what it looked like before the shooting. There were two two-by-fours."

"Was there anything you observed about this particular door that was unusual to you, sir?"

"It was, in my opinion. It was relatively new and wasn't consistent with the other doors in the building. There were six other apartment units altogether, and the other five had a different style of doors. This particular door had a large hole, maybe the diameter of a quarter beneath the peephole." Bradley said while holding the thumb of his right hand in a closed circle with his pointer finger.

"May I circulate all these photographs to the jury, Judge?" plaintiff's counsel requested as two jurors in the front row extended their hands.

"Yes, you may," Her Honor responded.

It wasn't enough to show the condition of the blue steel door, the presence of the two-by-fours, or the recently installed intercom. They all had to be connected to the landlords in a concrete way, showing what Campbell knew and when he knew it.

"Did you at some point interview Thomas Campbell?" Burke wanted to know.

"Yes, we tape-recorded a statement of Mr. Campbell at the homicide unit at 273 D Street in South Boston. We were trying to locate the person that rented the apartment on the third floor of Bellevue Street. His name was Delray Ferguson," Bradley explained as he produced a copy of a neatly typed eighteen-page transcript of the interview.

"Do you have a perfect memory of that interview?"

"Frankly, I don't."

"With the court's permission, may Captain Bradley use the statement to refresh his memory, Judge?"

The rules of evidence permit a witness who has forgotten a previous event to refresh his or her memory with a preexisting document, particularly when the statement was tape-recorded.

"Yes," Butler responded evenly as Lynch's chair creaked under his shifting weight.

"Did Mr. Campbell say if he ever met the tenant, this person Delray Ferguson?" Burke asked as the witness searched Campbell's statement for his response.

"Yes, Mr. Campbell said he never saw Delray, but there were other occupants up there he saw when he would go to collect the rents. Mr. Campbell told me, 'I would go up there and I would ask for Delray, and they kept saying he was out. They would say, "I am his cousin" or "his brother" and for me to come back. Later that evening they would have the money for me.'"

The jurors momentarily shifted their gaze from the witness to the landlords seated in the gallery and then back to Bradley.

"Did you ask Mr. Campbell if he recognized Albert Lewin's photograph?"

"Mr. Campbell said he had seen Lewin's picture in the paper and had seen Lewin three, four, maybe five times, between getting those three months' rent," the witness responded as he briefly glanced at the transcript.

"Did you ask Mr. Campbell when the intercom system was installed?"

"Yes," Bradley said, "he told me that an electrician by the name of Michael McDonald put it in about a week or two before the shooting. He told me that McDonald, the electrician, was only there one or two times. Mr. Campbell said the first time he noticed that a new door was put in there was somewhere around the middle or the end of January."

"So according to Mr. Campbell the new blue steel door and the intercom system are both installed approximately one or two weeks before the shooting of Sherman Griffiths?"

"Yes, Mr. Campbell told me the tenants installed the steel door."

Burke pulled back in mock shock. He turned to the jury while holding a picture of the interior of Lewin's cluttered living room and spoke without looking at the witness.

"Did you see any tools, a saw, a hammer, screwdriver, or a drill inside that apartment that could have been used to install that door?"

"No, sir. I didn't. I asked Mr. Campbell what his tenants did with the old door that was replaced, and he said he didn't know what happened to it. I also asked him about the hole in the door beneath the peephole, and Mr. Campbell said he didn't remember seeing the hole."

"Sir, do you know if that apartment even had heat in it?" Burke asked.

"No, it didn't. Mr. Campbell told me that three or four of the apartments had no heat in them."

"When you were done with the interview, did you play this tape recording back for Mr. Campbell to make any corrections he may have had?"

"Yes, I did, and he had no corrections," Bradley replied.

"I have no further questions for this witness," Burke announced as the attorney for the landlords replaced him at the end of the jury box.

COOPERATION

"Good morning, Captain." Frank Lynch smiled warmly as he rose from his chair.

"Good morning. How are you?" Bradley responded in kind.

"Is it fair to say that one of the major things you were trying to determine is who was present in the third-floor apartment at the time the shooting took place?"

"That's fair to say."

"There were no eyewitnesses from inside the apartment. So you didn't know if there were one or more individuals there at the time of the shooting, and whoever was inside there wasn't volunteering that information? You were trying to get witnesses, and that's why you interviewed Mr. Campbell?"

"That's correct," Bradley said. "We interviewed him at least one other time too. I think the night of the shooting."

"He was always cooperative, wasn't he?"

"Yes, sir," Bradley readily agreed.

"He responded to any requests the police department made of him and provided you with the name and telephone number of the electrician? He cooperated by telling you whether Lewin was occupying the premises at the time just prior to the shooting, correct?"

"Yes, sir. That's right."

"He provided you with all of his financial records relating to who was renting the apartment, didn't he?" Lynch asked.

"I don't believe he went that far. No, sir."

177

"OK, I don't want to argue with you, but when you seized those papers, you found out a Delray Ferguson lived there, and you went to my client, Mr. Campbell, to help you find him?"

"That's correct," Bradley said.

"One of the other people who gave you information was James McConnell, because McConnell was in the building the night of the shooting, right."

"That's right. McConnell wasn't arrested because he had slipped through the police lines that night."

"Now, according to Mr. Campbell, he had no knowledge of the installation of that steel door?" Lynch asked.

"That's what he stated to me."

"You never made any determination that any of the information Mr. Campbell gave you was incorrect, did you?"

"That's correct," Bradley replied.

"That's all I have. I appreciate your time. Thank you very much." Lynch smiled with a measured sense of self-satisfaction, knowing he had tipped the scale back.

"Thank you, Captain Bradley. We'll take the morning recess," Her Honor announced.

The bailiff simultaneously bellowed, "All rise."

SHIRLEY MCCONNELL

"You may call your next witness," Judge Butler stated crisply after she resumed her seat and the jurors had returned to their wooden enclosure from their lukewarm Dunkin' Donuts coffee, plain bagels, and cold cream cheese.

The plaintiff's lawyers had previously divided the responsibility for questioning the various witnesses in their case. It was now Newman's turn. He had made the trip to Dorchester early that morning to ensure Shirley McConnell's presence at the trial.

In fear of the Jamaicans, the witness would provide a rare insight into a drug dealer's world. She surveyed the courtroom for a friendly face, cautiously settled her eyes upon the police officer's widow, and then turned back to face the jury.

"Shirley, could you please state your name for the record?" Newman asked once the seamstress's daughter was sworn in.

"Shirley McConnell, M-c-C-o-n-n-e-l-l."

"Counsel, can I see you at the sidebar, please?" Her Honor asked suddenly, interrupting the flow.

"You'd have no way of knowing this, but the rule in my courtroom is, unless we're talking about children, we always refer to witnesses by their last name. Ms. McConnell," Judge Butler explained.

"I'm sorry, Judge," Newman apologized as he returned to plaintiff's table and began a second time.

"Ms. McConnell, are you dependent on drugs today? Are you testifying under the influence of any drug or unlawful narcotic?"

"No, sir," the witness responded with certainty in her voice.

It was always difficult to know what a jury thought of your witness, but there was an inescapable sense of redemption about the woman. A soul once lost in a drug-induced escape from the pains of her life, Shirley had crossed over. Arisen anew and buoyed by her faith, the witness told the court and the jury about the treatment programs that had restored her.

"I started out in Demi Street, as a detox patient. From Demi Street, I did First Incorporate, which is a nine-to-twelve-month program. I did the STAIR Program. I've done the Salvation Army program. Recently, I just graduated from Pine Street Transition House."

Burke watched intently as Shirley testified about her recovery and quietly wished Ruth was there, knowing she would be proud of the younger woman's journey back.

"Are you working?"

"I'm working for the AIDS Action Committee doing safety instruction on HIV and safe sex. I'm still going to school. I also do outreach work in the community and inform people about drug abuse."

It was an impressive résumé.

Newman took the witness back to Bellevue Street and her initial contact with the Jamaicans living in the third-floor apartment.

"When we first moved in, I wasn't aware of what was going on up on the third floor. It took about a month to find out they were dealing drugs up there. Several people I knew were going upstairs to buy drugs. So I started going up there myself to buy cocaine."

She told the rapt jury about her relationship with the Jamaican posse on the third floor, introducing them to the jurors by name, Star, Roddy, Smudge (Delray Ferguson), and Albert Lewin. Shirley described the desperate and constant flow of drug traffic, the initial process of dealing through an open door, and the attempts to rip off the Jamaican dealers, which led to their change to the stronger steel door with the pass-through hole. The witness confirmed the new door was secured by the two-by-fours shown in the photographs introduced through Captain Bradley.

A woman captured in the jaws of a cocaine death grip, Shirley's escape to sobriety brought with her the sense the jurors could believe what she told them. She calmly described her shadow of a life on Bellevue Street as the all-white jury looked on in stunned silence. It was all there, in the easy cadence of her soft voice. The witness knew everything about the posse. What kind of fast food the Jamaicans favored, where they kept their stash, and how they packaged their product. She admitted washing the dealers' clothes in exchange for coke and explained that her addiction grew voraciously, including smoking cocaine multiple times each day.

Her life was a spiraling descent into hell, interrupted only by the sound of a gunshot coming from the third floor.

"Now at some point, on the evening of February 17, 1988, did you hear the sound of a gun being fired?" Newman asked.

McConnell silently nodded about the moment that had altered her life.

"I was in my kitchen getting high. I didn't know what had happened upstairs, so I hid all my drug paraphernalia. That's when Albert Lewin came down the back stairs to my back door and I let him in. Albert had a gun, money, and some cocaine. The police were across the hall talking to another female tenant asking about the occupants on the third floor, and she told them to check my house. That's when the police came to my apartment."

The jurors leaned their bodies forward and craned their necks to hear Shirley describe the bedlam of the scene following the shooting.

"I took the money. My husband took the cocaine and the gun. I found out later James hid it under the mattress in our bedroom. Albert just went into the living room and sat down. That's when I went to the front door and let the police in. After they told me what happened on the third floor, I told them that Albert Lewin was the one that had come down from upstairs."

"Were you in fear of the Jamaicans?"

"Yes, I was. Very much so," the witness said, nodding.

"Now the person you've described as Smudge, Delray Ferguson. Did you ever see Mr. Campbell in the company of Smudge?"

"Yes, I seen them together a couple of times outside talking, but I have no idea what they were talking about."

"Your Honor, I have no further questions," Newman said, ending the inquiry.

Burke wondered in that moment why Sherman Griffiths died that cold February night and whether his death was related in any way to Shirley McConnell's redemption.

181

God brings people together for reasons we may never understand, Ruth's words repeated in Burke's mind just as the judge's voice broke the train of his thought.

"You may proceed with cross-examination," Her Honor said, nodding in the direction of defense counsel.

LOBBY CONFERENCE

Lynch knew there was damage to be repaired.

To undermine the witness's credibility, Lynch contended Shirley wasn't completely honest when she first spoke to the police in the presence of Albert Lewin.

"Would it be fair to say that the stories you told people on the evening of the shooting about what was going on at Bellevue Street consisted a little bit of lies and a little bit of truth?"

"Yes," Shirley acknowledged.

"You were trying to protect yourself, because you knew you were in trouble and you wanted to do whatever you could do to get out of trouble, didn't you?"

"Yes," she readily admitted.

"When you smoked your cocaine, what effect did it have on you?"

"It makes you paranoid, nervous."

"Would you be able to tell if you had smoked cocaine fifteen minutes earlier? Would *we* be able to tell?" Lynch asked as he turned toward the jury and the gallery while making a sweeping motion with his right hand and arm extended.

"No. Not on me. I don't know. I'd like to think you couldn't. I'll put it that way. On some people you can," the witness replied, measuring her own self-doubt.

Lynch saw an opportunity to diminish Shirley's ability to evaluate her own condition by using a portion of her previous deposition testimony to contradict her. It's called impeaching the witness with a prior inconsistent statement.

"Well, didn't you say before in your deposition that quote, 'I functioned normally. I mean if you came to my house, it was clean. I performed duties. Mentally I was well, but I still had a drug problem'?"

The jury waited for Shirley's response, and she turned directly toward them and began to speak.

"I lied. Because of the simple fact, I've been through several programs since I made that statement at my deposition. No, I did not function normally. I was not a normal person. At the time, I'm sure I liked to think I was, but I wasn't. I lied. I've learned a lot more about drugs and about myself since then."

"So what you are saying is despite the fact that you were sworn to tell the truth during your deposition, you were lying?"

"Objection," Burke said as Shirley spoke over him.

"That was the truth to me *then*, because I was in denial and denial *is* lying."

"Sustained," Her Honor chimed in belatedly, perhaps wishing for the moment she didn't need to make a ruling and could simply let the witness's answer stand.

"You're not exactly sure how long before the shooting that door was put in, are you?"

"I think around January or February."

"There hadn't been any holes in the other door, had there?"

"I don't remember. I just remember *this* door had it because that's how we transacted business."

"Were there two-by-fours behind the *old* door?"

"Just one, the new door had two."

"Now, you never told Mr. Campbell that these people were knocking on your window to get in and buy drugs on the third floor, did you?"

Lynch turned his body in a half circle, arcing back toward the gallery, gesturing to where the two landlords, Campbell and Bonnie Glenn, sat opposite Deirdre.

"No," the witness said forlornly, lowering her head as if in a confessional booth.

"You asked Mr. Campbell to fix the doorbell problem, and he fixed it, didn't he?"

"Yes," Shirley said with a compliant cadence to her voice.

"He did a number of repairs to the building while you were living there, and he was renovating some of the unoccupied units. He put in a new electrical system and an intercom system so you could speak to the person at the front door from your apartment, didn't he?"

"Yes."

Lynch was on a roll, demonstrating that his clients had earnestly attempted to improve the living conditions for their Bellevue Street tenants.

"Let me turn your attention to February 17, 1988. It was a pretty big event in your life, wasn't it?"

"Yes, it was."

"Now, when you heard the gunshot, you weren't really sure where anyone was. Your first reaction was to clean up your drug paraphernalia, correct?"

"Yes, I thought there was another robbery going on."

"Did you tell the police about the gun that night?"

"I don't remember if I did or not."

"Let me read your testimony from another trial. Question: 'Did you tell the police anything about a gun?' Your answer: 'No, not that night.' After the shooting, your daughter and your husband were still in the apartment. You didn't want anyone to know your husband was living there. You wanted to protect yourself, right?"

"Protect myself? I rented the apartment, that's why. I asked the police could my husband take my daughter out of the apartment. The house was full of police then."

"You never called the police to report that there was drug activity going on at Bellevue Street, and you never talked to Tom Campbell about anyone using drugs on the premises, did you?"

"No," Shirley said, slowly shaking her head.

"Thank you very much." Lynch smiled as he returned to his seat, accompanied by a nod of approval from his clients.

"OK. Thank you, Ms. McConnell. I'm going to give the jury a five-minute break. Can I see the attorneys at sidebar?" Her Honor asked as the four made the short walk next to the witness stand.

"With your permission, Counsel, and the jury won't be aware of this, but I would like to take a few minutes to talk to Ms. McConnell and ask

185

her about her drug recovery. It's just for my own purposes in terms of being a judge in criminal cases. It has nothing to do with this case."

"Sure." Burke nodded in approval of the informal lobby conference.

"OK," Lynch added.

The jurors made the quick trip from the courtroom to the jury room as the attorneys turned to the gallery in search of their respective clients. Once the fourteen citizens had cleared the courtroom, a burly court officer ushered Shirley into Her Honor's chambers.

"What did the judge ask you?" Deirdre wanted to know.

"She wanted to talk to Shirley about her recovery. I think she was impressed with how well she was doing," one of her lawyers explained.

"I'm so happy for her. That's so kind that the judge would do that," Griffiths's widow said with a smile.

It was a moment.

There was a haunting similarity between Shirley and the three women Burke had represented. Holly, Ruth, and Deirdre. All of them were burdened with a profound loss. Maybe Shirley's was self-inflicted, but she struggled along with the others, quietly searching for a reason to believe.

PAUL SCHROEDER

A former letter carrier, Paul Schroeder made the decision to leave the postal service and join the Boston Police Department out of respect and admiration for his two uncles. Both elder Schroeders were also Boston police officers who had been murdered in separate on-duty shootings years earlier. Schroeder had been assigned to the drug unit for a brief three months before the shooting of Sherman Griffiths.

Schroeder was the person closest to Sherm at the time the shots were fired from inside the apartment on the third floor.

He told the jurors he had traveled to the drug house on Bellevue Street in the same car with Sherman that evening. His assignment was to assist in the attempt to knock down the fortified door with a battering ram and a ten-pound sledgehammer. The ram was over four feet long, weighing more than thirty-five pounds, with a V-shaped head and handles on each side. Borrowed for the night from the Boston Fire Department, the device was designed for the sole purpose of taking down a door.

It was nearly eight p.m. on a cold, dark February evening when the police arrived at the drug house.

Dressed in heavy overcoats and casual street attire with their badges prominently displayed, two detectives went to the back of the building. The other four walked in the front door of the six-family unit, up two flights of stairs to the narrow landing on the third floor. Sherman was in the lead with Schroeder, Carlos Luna, and another detective following closely behind.

The witness described the fortified steel door to the jury, comparing it to the less secure wooden door in place months earlier when Detective

Rubin Colon readily seized the .38-caliber handgun and twenty-two packets of cocaine.

It was hushed in courtroom 10 as Newman's questions led Schroeder to the moment of death.

"I had the battering ram, and Sherman had the sledgehammer. We were going to use the ram, but the landing was too narrow for two men to use. Once Sherman yelled out, 'Police,' you could hear movement from inside the apartment. So I took the ram by myself and hit the door as hard as I could. I'm two hundred and fifteen pounds, but the door didn't move. The element of surprise was lost by then. I hit it probably six more times, and it still didn't move," Schroeder said, demonstrating for the jury.

"Can you tell us what happened next?" Newman asked softly as the jury leaned into the answer.

"I took a step back to take my gloves off and get a better grip on the battering ram, and Sherm moved forward toward the door. He yelled 'Police' again, and then hit the door three times with the sledgehammer. That's when the first shot rang out from inside the apartment."

Burke wasn't sure what to expect at that moment. He watched Schroeder's eyes turn to the back of the courtroom where Deirdre sat. She listened without movement, staring back, lost in the moment.

"Sherman fell directly to the floor, to the right-hand side. I saw blood on the wall. There was no movement from him. That's when I drew my revolver and fired back in the door. Then there were three other shots fired back at us from inside the apartment," the witness said as he glanced back to the gallery again.

He paused long enough to clear his throat.

"I stayed there on the landing with Sherman until the EMTs arrived."

It was an unspoken comfort for Deirdre to know that Paul Schroeder had been with her husband as he lay amid the scattered lottery slips, dying on the cold, dirty floor of the drug house at 102–104 Bellevue Street.

RODNEY BLACK

He had been away from home for a few months.

A drug dealer and runner for the crew on the third floor of the Bellevue Street apartment, Rodney O'Neill Black was on a bumpy road to recovery when he took the stand to testify about the Jamaicans and the murder of Sherman Griffiths. Born into a life of crime, with few options, the witness wore his years on the street like a heavy, thick overcoat.

The normal procedure for the introduction of a witness to the jury was to ask questions about their employment, education, or family history.

"Where's your domicile? Where do you live?" Newman asked as the witness shifted uncomfortably in the leather seat facing the jury.

"At this moment, I'm incarcerated at the Dedham House of Correction for larceny," Black explained.

There was no subtlety, no way getting around who their witness was or what he had previously done. With a pedigree of not-so-petty offenses, the best approach was to simply tell the jury about it before the other side got the chance.

"Do you have a previous criminal record for other crimes?"

"Yes, I do. They're mostly larcenies, shoplifting, and one possession of cocaine with intent to distribute," the witness explained as he turned to his left toward the jury enclosure.

"Have there been any promises made to you for testifying here today?" Newman asked.

"No," Black declared softly with a shake of his head.

"I want to direct your attention to a particular group operating in the Dorchester section of Boston in '85, '86. Did you connect yourself in some way with this criminal group?"

"Yes, I did. It was the Jamaican posse. They were involved in all different kind of crimes, and I was one of the drug dealers working with them. I first worked for them over on Geneva Avenue. Then we moved over to 102–104 Bellevue Street," the witness said, readily acknowledging his role in the sale of cocaine.

"What did you do for them there?"

"I ran, like, sales. I ran the doors."

"What were the names of some of the people that you worked with at Bellevue Street?" Newman asked.

"There was Star, Smudge, and Bird. Smudge was a captain, like in charge," the witness offered, barely above a whisper.

Two of the jurors nodded at Black's mention of the names Star and Smudge, as though they were a recent acquaintance.

"Mr. Black, please keep your voice loud enough so that all of the jurors can hear you," Judge Butler said.

Rodney nodded. "All right," he said, followed by an inaudible apology to the jurors.

"I'd like you to describe to the court and jury the type of traffic that went into Bellevue Street while you were working there."

"Mainly drug users in and out, all races. Twenty-four hours a day, seven days a week," Rodney explained matter-of-factly.

Burke watched the jurors as the flow of information washed over them. While some jurors may have had a passing exposure to drugs at some level, he was certain that few, if any, had ever seen the inside of a drug house.

"Can you recall how much money was brought in by this drug trade each day?"

"Depends on which day it was. Mondays through Wednesdays, say a thousand a day. Thursday, Friday, Saturday, Sundays, from three to four thousand, all cash."

"Were the drugs packaged in a certain way?" Newman asked.

"Yeah, either in Baggies or lottery slips, Megabucks papers," Black said, mimicking the wrapping motion necessary to secure the coke inside.

"What part of the apartment did they deal out of?"

"At one time, I used to open the door, and then they started dealing it through a hole in the front door."

"Did you ever see the Jamaicans physically change the door there?" Newman asked.

"No, I didn't," he told the jury, shaking his head negatively.

Burke hoped that Black's answer led the jury to ask themselves. "If the Jamaicans didn't install the new blue steel door, then who did?"

It was important for the plaintiff to prove the drug dealers hadn't installed the reinforced steel door themselves. They had no tools. The finished wood trim surrounding the door with mitered edges indicated someone with a carpenter's experience did the work.

The topic moved quickly to another event with a more certain outcome.

"Now, if I could, Mr. Black, I'd like to direct your attention to an incident on June 16, 1987. Do you recall doing something in that third-floor apartment?"

"Yes," Rodney said slowly as he defensively moved his hand toward his abdomen.

"What did you do in that apartment?"

"I got tired of the Jamaicans and robbed them." The witness gestured, as if pointing to the absent drug dealers. "I put a gun to them and robbed them of their coke and money."

"Then the next day, June 17, 1987, do you recall being on Bowdoin Street?"

"Yes. Bowdoin is about a half mile from Bellevue Street, takes three minutes to walk there."

"What happened on Bowdoin Street?"

"I was shot," Black said without emotion, pulling his hand closer to his stomach while the jurors cringed.

"Did you recognize the person that shot you?"

"Yeah, it was Star, one of the Jamaicans who operated out of Bellevue Street. I was standing in front of a Chinese restaurant ordering some Chinese food, me and a friend. I noticed someone hopping out of a car, which was Star. He walked up toward me, fired one shot. I pulled away from it. He missed and then fired another shot and hit me in the stomach, but I didn't go down 'til I noticed I got shot. I walked through the alley; then I passed out."

"Do you recall giving a statement to the police and telling them who shot you and where they were?" Newman asked.

"Yes, I did."

"Do you have a memory of what kind of gun was used to shoot you?"

"Yes, it was a .45 automatic. The Jamaicans used to keep the gun in the apartment on Bellevue Street."

"Was the person who shot you ever arrested?"

"Yes, he pled guilty and was incarcerated."

"Now, just to backtrack a bit, did the members of the posse operating out of Bellevue Street drive cars?"

"Yes, they drove Sterlings and Maximas," Black said, explaining the connection between the British-made Sterlings and the island of Jamaica.

"What was the condition of the third-floor apartment?" the plaintiff's lawyer asked, contrasting the expense of the Sterlings with the drab conditions of the third floor.

"Run down, beat up."

"Did you know a person by the name of Shirley McConnell?"

"Yes, she lived on the first floor. She was mainly a runner. She would find customers, run back, get the coke, and then bring it back to them, back and forth," Black explained, using his hand in a pantomime of running up and down the stairs.

"I have no further questions," Newman said as he took his seat.

RECORDS OF CONVICTION

Lynch knew how to try a case. He quickly made his way to the end of the jury box with a large stack of official-looking documents and a yellow legal pad full of notes. It was just before three in the afternoon on a mild seventy-degree day with the air conditioner running.

"Good afternoon, Mr. Black," Lynch said warmly.

"Good afternoon," the witness responded cautiously.

"Now, Mr. Newman mentioned at the beginning of his examination that you've been convicted of numerous crimes, correct?"

"Yes, I have."

Lynch held the papers stamped with a large red seal directly in front of him for the benefit of the jury as he asked the next series of questions.

The rules of evidence allow a party to introduce a witness's prior records of conviction to impeach the credibility of their testimony. As if currently living in the Dedham House of Corrections wasn't enough.

"You've been convicted of a number of crimes in Dorchester District Court, and a number of crimes in Suffolk Superior Court, right?"

"Yes, I have."

"You've been convicted of crimes in the Waltham District Court and Quincy District Court also?"

"Yes, for larceny."

"You've been convicted of a number of crimes in the Cambridge District Court?" Lynch asked, adding to his list of cities and towns where the witness had made an appearance.

"Yes, for larceny."

"How about the East Boston District Court?"

"I don't remember that."

"Assault and battery on a public servant?" the lawyer suggested in an attempt to refresh Black's memory.

"Oh yeah, I remember that. I was incarcerated for that crime."

"You were convicted in the Boston Municipal Court too, weren't you? That's the building next to the new courthouse in Pemberton Square."

"Yes, I was."

When he was finished, Lynch offered Black's stack of records of convictions as a single exhibit, handing them in a neat collection for the clerk to mark. It took all of a minute to go through the small mound of documents. Defense counsel watched the jurors make their own count in sequence with the clerk before moving on.

"Now, after your shooting in June of 1987, you were interviewed by a Boston detective named John Arnstein to prosecute the individual who allegedly shot you, correct?"

"Yes."

"Did you tell Detective Arnstein that you bought drugs at Bellevue Street and that you were an employee, inside selling drugs there?"

"No, I did not tell him either of those things."

"He asked you what your involvement was at Bellevue Street, didn't he?"

"No, he did not. He didn't ask me whether I bought drugs or sold drugs in that same building."

"Didn't he ask you why the individual shot you?"

"Yes, he asked me why."

"I'm just trying to make it clear. You're telling us today that you robbed Star, but when Arnstein interviewed you, he didn't ask you what you did at Bellevue Street to get yourself shot?"

"He might have, but I don't recall telling him I robbed Star. No, I never told them that, because they was a cop. Why would I tell a cop I was a purchaser or a drug dealer at a coke house?" Black asked rhetorically, attempting to sort it out for the jury and himself.

"Are you denying today that you told him that?"

"No, not deny it. There's a good chance I would have, but I don't think I would have told him that." Black said with uncertainty.

"But you're clear that you didn't tell Arnstein that you were either a buyer or seller of drugs at Bellevue Street, right?"

"Yeah, I'm clear. I'm definitely sure about that."

"Now a couple of years later, in 1989, after Officer Griffiths was shot, you had a different interview with two detectives from the Boston police homicide unit, and you told them the gun that shot you was the same gun used to shoot Sherman Griffiths. Is that correct?"

"Yes."

"You came forward with that information because you expected it would help you with the Boston police, didn't you?"

"No."

"You just did it on your own accord?"

"Yes, because I wasn't in trouble then."

"You're telling me now that you weren't interested in getting any help from the Boston police in exchange for that information?"

"No, I probably did it out of paranoia, if anything, being scared of the police."

"Well, you were arrested both before that interview and after that interview. You understand that sometimes cooperating with the police can help you with the consequences of being arrested?"

"No, because it never happened with me."

"But you did tell the police in 1989 that you were a purchaser of drugs at Bellevue Street?" Lynch said, comparing the denial made two years earlier to John Arnstein.

"Yeah, that's what's in the statement, yes."

"You also told the homicide detectives in 1989 that the doorman in that third-floor apartment was Albert Lewin, didn't you?"

"Yes."

"But isn't it your testimony here today, sir, that you never went back to Bellevue Street after you were shot in June of 1987?" Lynch asked.

"Yes, I never went back there."

"Well, sir, Albert Lewin didn't become the so-called doorman at the apartment at Bellevue Street until months after you were shot, not until sometime in December of 1987 or January of 1988."

"I don't know, because I wasn't there."

"But you told the police officers in this statement that Albert Lewin was the door—"

"Right," Black agreed. "Yes, Albert Lewin. I saw it on the news. That's where I got the name."

195

"So then, to be of help to the police, you knew they wanted information that would implicate Albert Lewin for this crime, correct?"

"I didn't try to implicate Albert Lewin to the crime."

"Putting him there as the doorman at Bellevue Street didn't implicate him in anything?" Lynch asked.

"No."

"You never told the homicide detectives about your involvement at Bellevue Street until December 1989, almost two years after Officer Griffiths was shot, correct?"

"Yes."

"Give me a minute, Your Honor," Lynch said while reviewing the notes on his legal pad.

"Nothing further of this witness," he added.

"Do you have anything on redirect?" Her Honor inquired of plaintiff's counsel.

"No further questions," Newman responded, dismounting from the three-legged horse.

THOMAS CAMPBELL

Civil cases are different from criminal trials. A prosecutor in a criminal case can't call the defendant as a witness or even mention their failure to testify. Not so in a civil case. As a plaintiff in a civil suit, you are permitted to call the defendant as your own witness and cross-examine them.

It was September 6 and midafternoon on the first day of the trial. The jury had already heard testimony from the four previous witnesses as Burke called for Thomas Campbell.

There was a risk in calling Campbell as a witness in the presentation of Deirdre's case. The forty-four-year-old accountant and part-time landlord would be difficult to control on the stand. He was college educated, articulate, and not necessarily what the jurors had pictured from the opening statements. Pleasant in appearance, dressed appropriately in a conservative suit, white shirt, and striped tie, the defendant made his way to the witness stand to the left of Judge Butler.

Burke took his usual position at the far end of the jury box, alternating his eyes from the witness to the jurors and back again.

"Good afternoon, Mr. Campbell," Her Honor said as the witness raised his right hand.

"Good afternoon," Campbell responded with an agreeable smile.

The examination began with the usual preliminary questions concerning Campbell's business relationship with Bonnie Glenn, the proximity of their office to the apartment at Bellevue Street, and the home inspection done of the property by a building inspector named Harry Gottschalk.

"Did Mr. Gottschalk inform you that ownership of this building would require constant attention?" Burke asked while holding the inspection report aloft.

"Yes," the landlord acknowledged.

"He told you that there are 'social problems' in the area. Did you interpret the social problems in any way to be construed as drugs in that house?"

"Not particularly, no. Not then."

"Well, did you do any background investigation on the tenants in the building you were about to buy, where they worked or their history of rent payment?"

"No, I didn't."

"Can you tell me what, if any, visible means of support the individuals occupying the third-floor apartment had?" Burke asked.

"At the time, I never met the tenant up there."

"The fact that you owned this building for eleven months before the shooting of Sherman Griffiths and during that time never met the tenant, didn't that raise your suspicion about who was living there?"

"Objection," defense counsel asserted.

"Overruled," Her Honor said to Lynch.

"Yes, it did," Campbell said. "I was trying to find the tenant in there. His name was Delray Ferguson."

"Well, you said you collected rents there on an almost monthly basis. Do you recall writing out a receipt in your own hand for four hundred dollars from one Delray Ferguson, shortly after you took possession of that property?"

"I don't recall writing a receipt, no."

"Well, you were frequently in that building, weren't you, during that first eleven months? And you put in a new intercom system but never did any major improvements to that apartment, right?" Burke asked.

"Yes, in the beginning I was in the building two or three times a week, doing repair work, cosmetic type stuff."

"And during that eleven months, you collected rents from a number of different people in that third-floor apartment. Didn't that raise your suspicions, sir, when you went there and it was three of four different people who were paying you the rent money in cash for that occupancy?"

"Yes, it did. I kept asking for Delray Ferguson. They would tell me, 'I'm his brother,' or 'I'm his cousin.'"

"When they would open the door, did that give you a vantage point to see the interior of that apartment?"

"Yes, some of it, but not all of it," Campbell said, gesturing with both hands to making a narrow angle of opening. "It was sparsely furnished."

"Well, it wasn't just sparsely furnished. It was sparsely heated, wasn't it?" Burke retorted.

"Yes, there was a space heater up there."

"After you raised the rent for them, did you put heat up there?"

"No, I didn't."

"There were times when you went there in the morning to collect the rent and they gave you part of it, and you would come back in the very same afternoon and they would give you the balance, right?"

"Could be. I'm not sure. I don't recall exactly if I was there in the afternoon or the next day."

"Well, did you ever question where their money came from?"

"No, I did not."

"Did you care, sir, who it was that was occupying your property during the two years before you sold it?"

"Yes, of course," Campbell said in his most earnest voice.

"You saw the brackets for the two-by-fours, right? Did that increase your suspicions?"

"No, it did not. No, it did not," Campbell repeated for emphasis.

"Well, you sure didn't see any big-screen TV or expensive oriental rugs or any large amounts of cash in there, did you?"

"No. I wouldn't expect to."

"Well after Albert Lewin told you he put this new steel door up for security purposes, did you question in your mind what he was trying to protect inside that apartment?"

"No."

"Had any other tenants put up any steel doors?" Burke asked.

"Not doors, no."

"I show you this check stub in your handwriting, written approximately three weeks before Sherman Griffiths was killed. It's made out to a Mr. Thad Bird, in the amount of four hundred and fifty dollars for the installation of two doors. Isn't one of them the steel door on the third floor?"

"No, he was a gentleman who installed two doors for me on the second floor. Both were wooden doors. I wanted metal doors. That's why I never used him again."

199

"Well, do you have a work order for these two doors?"

"I can go back to the office and look for it," Campbell deflected.

"There was a new door installed at your direction on the second floor, right?"

"Yes. I am not sure why I had that one replaced," Campbell said as he searched the check stub for an answer.

"And the new door on the second floor has molding with mitered edges. It's a finished product, isn't it?"

"Yes."

"Now looking at the photographs of the door that suddenly appears on the third floor, doesn't that have the *same* type of trim work, with mitered edges?"

"Somewhat finished. It's not..." Campbell attempted to make a distinction while he held both pictures aloft.

"Judge, may I just circulate this photograph to the jury?" Burke asked while handing an eight-by-eleven glossy of the third-floor steel door to the nearest juror.

"Yes," Her Honor said with a nod.

"Well, Mr. Campbell, when you said you went up to the third floor and discovered a new door there, did you ever offer to reimburse your tenant for improving your premises?"

"At that time, no." Campbell squirmed and reached to loosen his striped tie.

"Well, did you thank him for putting a new door in for you?"

"No. I asked him why the door was up there. He told me someone had broken into his apartment, and he had to replace the door. I said I needed a key, and he gave me one."

"Did you ever ask Mr. Lewin if he made an insurance claim for property damage or anything that was stolen out of that apartment?"

"No, I did not."

"Did *you* file an insurance claim as a result of this door being kicked in?"

"No."

"Based on your experience, sir, did you see a single solitary thing inside that apartment worth stealing?" Burke asked and simultaneously shook his head before the answer was given.

"No," Campbell said, glancing at his own lawyer for direction.

"Did you ask him why he had the other hole in the door that allowed things to be passed from the outside to the inside?"

"No. I did not. I only remember one peephole in that door. There might have been, but I don't remember seeing it. I'm not saying it couldn't have been there. I just don't recall seeing it."

"Did you find it curious, unusual, or somehow spark your interest that the new door didn't have a door handle on it? A doorknob?"

"At the time, no. No."

"How many *other* doors in your building didn't have a doorknob?"

"None of them."

"How many *other* doors had two holes?" Burke asked.

"None of them, I believe."

"Well, were you aware of a police raid on your property when a police officer by the name of Ruben Colon took a .38-caliber gun and twenty-two packets of cocaine out of that third-floor apartment?"

"Objection," Lynch said, rising quickly from his chair.

"Overruled," Judge Butler disagreed.

"I…I had no knowledge of that," Campbell asserted.

"Did Mr. McDonald ever tell you he had bought drugs there or that there was rampant drug dealing and heavy foot traffic in and out of there?"

"No, he did not."

"Well, do you recall an incident when a man came to your office with a number of gold chains and a big wad of cash and paid your partner, Bonnie Glenn, the rent for the third-floor apartment?"

"Yes, I do, but I don't know if the chains were *real* gold."

"Well, the wad of cash was real, right?"

"Yes, I guess."

"Did that raise your suspicions?" Burke asked.

"Raise my suspicions? I was curious, yes."

"Besides being curious, were you suspicious?"

"Yes."

"Well, you knew there was no visible means of support for any of the four or five people who were occupying that apartment, didn't you?"

"Yes."

"You were suspicious that they were drug dealers, weren't you?"

"No, I was not."

"Well, you knew they weren't selling Good Humor Ice Cream out front, didn't you?

"No," Campbell answered meekly.

"Objection," Lynch complained.

"Sustained," Her Honor agreed.

Burke was about to ask another question when the judge raised her right hand.

"This seems to be a good place to stop for the day," she explained. "Jurors, please do not discuss the case with each other or with anyone else. I'll see you tomorrow. Thank you."

The fourteen citizens smiled and nodded in agreement as the bailiff led them out of courtroom 10.

It had been a long first day.

COURT SIDE CAFÉ

Located just off High Street, less than a hundred yards from the courthouse, the Court Side Café was a tiny hole-in-the-wall set six granite steps down from the busy street leading into Dedham center. The joint was your typical greasy spoon, with daily blue-plate specials, wafer-thin paper napkins, and heavy, off-white-colored porcelain plates and cups. The place featured a small grouping of 1950s-era booths, set across from a narrow food counter with round, red stationary stools that stretched the length of the room. The breakfast menu choices in the crowded eatery were limited, but the service was quick, intended to encourage a "chew and screw" mentality for its patrons.

It was late morning and another pleasant early-September day as the two lawyers sat at the counter of the Court Side with their eggs over easy, toast, and orange juice. The room was awash with lawyers and court personnel from the probate, district, and superior courts adjoining the tiny restaurant. The legal industry was in full bloom.

"Did you get any sleep last night, Timothy?" Newman offered between bites.

"Not much. You?"

"Same. I'm just worried this jury won't want to hold the landlords responsible for what some drug dealers did on their property."

"It really does come down to what we can prove they knew about what was going on inside their building, doesn't it?"

"Yeah, Timothy, in some ways, it's just that simple."

The lawyers finished quickly, as required, walked back to the domed courthouse, and took their places at their designated table as the jurors were led back into the courtroom. The assembled group stood in unison as

203

the court officer gave the "All rise" just before Her Honor's entrance from the left side of the ornate bench.

"Mr. Campbell, you may resume the stand." Judge Butler gestured as the clerk reminded the witness he was still under oath.

"Do you recognize this photograph as the front entrance to 102–104 Bellevue Street?" Burke began quickly as he faced the jury and held up an exhibit introduced the previous day.

"Yes."

The goal of effective cross-examination is to limit the type of response a witness can make. Each question was asked with the intention of requiring either a yes or no response. Burke seldom asked someone on the other side of a case to explain his or her answer or an opened-ended question that allowed the witness to offer an opinion. It's called keeping the witness on a short leash.

"And to the right of the doorway is an intercom?" Burke pointed.

"Yes."

"When was the intercom installed?"

"December of '87," Campbell answered.

"So about a month and a half before Sherman Griffiths was murdered?"

"Yes."

"So, you had several new doors going in your building right around the middle of January of 1988. There are apparently three new doors. You had the one on the first floor, the entrance to the building; one on the second floor; and then another one on the third floor where Sherman Griffiths was shot and killed, right?"

"Yes," Campbell agreed.

"You told the jurors yesterday that you never noticed the second hole in the door on the third-floor apartment, even though you were up there a number of times to collect the rents when Albert Lewin was there, didn't you?"

"Yes."

It was early morning on the second day of the trial and time to confront the witness with an issue Burke believed Campbell was lying about. In some ways the case hung in the moment.

"You'd come up the stairs, walk down this hall, and bang on the door, correct?" the lawyer asked, pantomiming the steps taken by Campbell and the knocks on the steel door.

"Yes," the witness responded.

"And the peephole, because it is a peephole, it's positioned at almost eye level, isn't it?" Burke asked as he held his right hand in a horizontal position in front of his eyes.

"Yes, it is."

"How tall are you, sir?"

"Almost six feet."

"Would your eye level have been about the same height as the peephole as you knocked on the door to collect the rent from these individuals?"

"Yes, that's correct."

"You're telling this jury here today that you never saw this second hole underneath the peephole as you knocked on the door to collect the rent from Albert Lewin on some four or five occasions?"

"Yes, that's correct," Campbell repeated with less certainty.

"Sir, isn't the reason you're saying you never saw this second hole is because it's obvious to anyone with a modicum of common sense that it was being used as a pass-through hole?"

"Objection," the landlord's attorney said, rising quickly from his chair.

"Overruled," Butler responded evenly while the jurors turned back to the witness.

"I'm not sure what the question was," Campbell said, explaining his hesitation as Lynch resumed his seat.

"The fact is, sir, you're denying being aware of that pass-through hole—"

"I really didn't—"

"—when it is obvious to anyone with a modicum of common sense that it was being used to pass money through and drugs out?"

"Objection, Your Honor," Lynch tried again.

"Overruled," the judge repeated.

"I recall one peephole, that's all."

"Now, sir, you knew there was another drug raid at your building six months before Sherman Griffiths was killed, wasn't there? The incident when the Boston police found a gun and 22 packets of cocaine?"

"No, I didn't."

"Isn't it a fact you're denying knowing about that drug raid at your building because it would have put you on notice of the illegal activity in the building that you owned?"

"No, I am not."

Burke hesitated before he asked the next question, allowing the jury a moment to consider Campbell's previous answer.

"You told the jurors that you installed an intercom system in late December?"

"Yes, that's correct."

"Sir, isn't it a fact that the reason you installed the intercom system is because one of your tenants complained to you about all the foot traffic going up to the third floor?"

"Shirley McConnell complained to me about some people knocking on her window, trying to get into the apartment when the door was locked."

"Didn't that raise your suspicions who these people were and why they were knocking on her window in the middle of December? It's cold out, isn't it?"

"Yes, it is. I would think so."

"Did you *prioritize* the installation of an intercom system over the need for putting heat in the apartment on the third floor?" Burke asked.

"Yes."

"Didn't the Boston Gas Company come to you and complain about the unlawful use of unmetered gas on the third floor of that apartment?"

"I believe they did, yes."

"When Boston Gas complained about the unlawful use of unmetered gas, did you take any steps to evict your tenants from the third floor? Whoever those tenants might have been?"

"No, I did not. I thought Delray Ferguson would come out of the woodwork. I'd been trying to contact him to find out who he was. So, if there was no heat, he would have to come to complain to me."

Burke paused again to gauge the jury's reaction.

"You told the jurors that you didn't do any background or employment checks of your tenants. Did you care, sir, where they got their money as long as their rent on time?"

"Well, most of them were on either on welfare or—"

"Yes or no, sir. Did you care what their source of income was as—"

"Not really, no."

"Let me finish please...as long as they paid the rent on time?"

206

"Not really."

"You didn't really care, did you?" Burke asked.

"I would have to say no."

"You never met or even spoke to Delray Ferguson while he was a tenant of yours, did you?"

"No, I did not."

"Let me show you this tenant ledger, sir. It's your record of payments for the *tenants* on the third floor of your building for the months of January and February of 1988, isn't it?" Burke said as he approached the witness stand with the neatly printed ledger.

"Yes, it is."

"Does it indicate from whom you received four hundred and fifty dollars in cash for the rent?"

"Delray Ferguson."

"The guy you never met or spoke to, right?"

"Ah, yeah."

Campbell hesitated and slowly pushed the ledger away from his body as Burke inched closer.

"You'd go there in the morning and collect part of the rent and then come back later on in the afternoon and get the rest of it. You'd get an envelope with cash in it, right?"

"I wouldn't get an envelope. It was just loose bills."

"Oh, OK. That money came from Delray, even though you had no idea who he was?"

"Right."

"Yesterday, I asked you about the work order for the doors that were installed. Have you been able to locate them?" Burke asked.

"No. I couldn't locate them. I spent last night trying to find a receipt, but I couldn't."

"OK, going back to the conversation that you had with Albert Lewin. You first learned about this door around February 1 when you went to collect the rent, right?"

"About then, yes."

"He told you somebody had broken in?"

"Yes."

"Did you ask Mr. Lewin if he filed a police report?"

"I don't recall," Campbell said.

"Did you ask Mr. Lewin what of value was missing from that apartment?"

"I don't recall whether I did or not."

"Did you ever ask Mr. Lewin to take that door down?"

"No, I didn't."

"If you didn't want that door there, you certainly had the authority to have it taken down, didn't you?"

"Yes, I did."

"Given your educational experience, were you aware that drug dealing is an activity that creates the risk of harm to third parties in and around the area of the drug dealing?"

"I would have to say yes."

"And you know that drug dealers frequently have guns?"

"Yes."

"Did you know then, sir, during your ownership of this building, that drug dealers frequently use force and violence—"

"Yes—"

"—to protect themselves, their turf, their product, cocaine, heroin, and crack?"

"Yes."

"And you knew when you bought that property, if a landlord was aware of drug dealing inside, the building could be forfeited, didn't you?"

"Objection," the landlord's attorney stated with a pitched voice.

"Overruled," Her Honor responded.

"I was told that later, yes. Not at the time I owned the property."

"You weren't in fear of the occupants of that third-floor apartment, were you?"

"No."

"Nothing further," Burke told the court and jury before returning to counsel table with Newman.

Both of Deirdre's attorneys turned to their right to see what Lynch would do with his examination. He was a sophisticated lawyer who saw all the issues in a case and knew how to combat the negative inferences created against his clients.

*****

208

"Mr. Campbell, you learned about the so-called forfeiture law at some point, didn't you?" Lynch began.

"Yes, I found out about it a couple of years after the incident had occurred."

"You didn't take any courses on the legal rights of landlords and tenants when you were back in college twenty years ago, did you?"

"No, I did not, sir," the witness responded evenly.

"You don't believe people have the right to do illegal drugs, do you?"

"No, I do not," Campbell said with a thin note of indignation.

"If you saw someone committing an illegal act, what would you do?"

"Well, first, I would have contacted my partner, Bonnie. Then I would have called the police."

Lynch switched the inquiry to Campbell's background in an attempt to project a positive image.

"Can you tell us a little about yourself, sir?"

"I grew up in the suburbs of Boston, graduated from high school, spent one semester at Bentley College, and was drafted during the Vietnam War. In lieu of being drafted, I enlisted in the army in 1971. I was in the service for three years, honorably discharged, and then continued my education at the University of Massachusetts in Lowell. I graduated with a bachelor of science degree in 1979."

"What did you do after that?" Lynch asked, knowing he was scoring points with the jury.

"I got a job working in an accounting firm. I became a CPA, a certified public accountant. I am still an accountant today. To become a CPA, you need to pass a very grueling test and fill out an application with letters of reference, statements attesting to your credibility, your ethics, all signed under the pains and penalties of perjury. I satisfied all those requirements in 1990."

Campbell was a more relaxed witness while explaining his background. His lawyer's questions provided the jury with a chance to see another side of the witness's personality. Throughout the proceedings the accountant was unfailingly polite to both sides.

"Now can you explain your connection to the Bellevue Street property?"

"At some point, Bonnie approached me and asked if I would be interested in buying the property on Bellevue together. I didn't have any money for the down payment. She was going to provide the down payment, and I would handle the management of the property, collect the rents, and supervise whatever renovations we were going to do."

"So when Mr. Burke asked you if *you* had interviewed the tenants, that wasn't your job, was it?"

"No, it was Bonnie's job to do that."

"Did you ever communicate with the people living there?"

"After we bought the building, I sent out a form letter to all of the holdover tenants. I also introduced myself to the ones that were there about what their rent was and how to pay it. I didn't want to be collecting rents. I wanted them to mail the rent or come down to our office to pay it with checks or money orders."

"That didn't work out, did it?"

"No. Some tenants didn't have checking accounts. And a money order cost two or three dollars, so they would rather pay cash. It was easier for them, after they cashed their welfare or social security checks."

The jury sat listening intently as Lynch dealt with each of the topics raised over the course of the previous two days.

"Now did you receive a response from the form letter you sent to Delray Ferguson?"

"No, I did not. So I went to the apartment to speak to Mr. Ferguson. I knocked on the door. I don't know who came to answer, but I explained I was the new landlord and asked them to have him get in touch with me, but there was no response."

"You were present here in court when you heard Captain Bradley testify about the statement you gave the police. That was before this lawsuit was brought, correct?"

"Yes, I told the police that I would go to the door and a number of different individuals would answer and explain to me they were related to Delray, that he wasn't present, and he'd get back to me. I made a pest of myself looking for Delray Ferguson because he owed rent," Campbell explained, offering a logical explanation for the tenant's absence.

"Now, when you bought the property, there was an inspection report done by Mr. Harry Gottschalk, correct?"

"There were many problems with the building, especially the third-floor apartment. There wasn't a heater in each room, just a gas heater in the

210

living room, which was the tenant's responsibility to pay for. They were on a separate meter. The gas company would send the tenant the bill. It was the same thing for the electric bill."

"So, if the heat was off, the tenant would presumably want to do something about it, correct?"

"I would think so, yes," the witness readily agreed, providing another perfectly logical explanation for the lack of heat to the third-floor apartment.

"Mr. Burke asked you whether you ever attempted to evict Delray Ferguson. I want to show you this document he marked as an exhibit, a notice to quit, correct?" Lynch asked, gaining steam.

"It's a notice for Mr. Ferguson to vacate the unit, to leave for nonpayment of rent. The notice was given to a constable, who served it in hand to Delray Ferguson. After he received that notice, the rent was paid."

"You had to chase other tenants in the building for rent too, didn't you?"

"Yes, it was an ongoing process, chasing down ten dollars here, a hundred dollars there. That's one of the reasons I wanted Section 8 tenants in the building. Because the checks come directly from the government to the office, so I don't have to chase people for rent money."

"OK. So after you introduced yourself to the tenants and got everyone current on rent, what did you do next to the building?"

"We looked at Mr. Gottschalk's inspection report. My first concern was the electrical and fire issues. So I had the service upgraded from a sixty-amp service to four hundred amps, all new wiring. We put in new hard-wired smoke detectors. I hired an electrician by the name of Michael McDonald to do that and bring it up to code," the witness explained to the jury, some of whom politely nodded as if in agreement with the improvements.

"What else did you do in those first few months to the building?"

"Well, we had an exterminator come in. The mailboxes needed to be fixed. All the locks needed to be replaced. We had to fix the hot water tank in Shirley McConnell's apartment. We installed new exterior floodlights, front and back, for safety and security reasons. Stripped wall paper and hired a contractor to do some painting. Then we renovated an empty unit with a new kitchen sink, cabinets, new stove, new toilet and sink. Later on we put in new handrails on the front and back steps. There were many little things we did."

Lynch was doing a good job at restoring the jury's image of his client by having Campbell go through a month-by-month breakdown of the improvements made to 102–104 Bellevue Street.

"So from March of 1987, when you bought the building, until that September, how much money had been spent in repairs?"

"We spent about nineteen thousand dollars for that time period and then another two thousand dollars for the next three months after that for the intercom system."

"Did you plan to renovate the other units in the building?"

"Yes, within the first two years. We wanted to do all the units, including Mr. Ferguson's."

"Now, let's see if we can straighten out the door issue. Mr. Burke asked you about the two doors you wrote out a check for on January 20, 1988, correct?"

"Yes, I wrote a note on the check stub, 'Two doors O/S' and '104-2'. The 'O/S' stands for the outside door, and the '104-2' means apartment number 2 on the 104 side, second floor. I told the contractor I wanted metal-clad doors in there, but he didn't do it. That's why I never used him again."

"Now, the other door that Mr. Burke discussed with you was the one on the third floor?"

"Yes, the bluish-gray door that Mr. Lewin or someone up there installed, yes, I do," Campbell agreed as if it were a distant occurrence.

"Mr. Burke asked you when that confrontation with Mr. Lewin took place. It was a couple of weeks before the shooting, correct?"

"Yes."

"That's when you saw a new door had been put in place, correct?"

"Yes, I went to collect the rent."

"When I first saw the door, I remember asking him for a key to the door. Lewin said, 'No problem.' At some point I went back there again to get the key, and it worked."

"You didn't go there and knock on that door four or five times after that, did you?"

"No, no," the witness responded eagerly.

"So when Mr. Burke asked you how many times you went to the door on the third floor to collect the rents from Mr. Lewin, and you said four or five times, you were talking about the first four or five times from when Mr. Lewin first started to appear."

"Yes, yeah." Campbell nodded in sync with Lynch.

"You were asked about this peephole by Mr. Burke. And you were asked about it by Captain Bradley in 1989, weren't you?"

"Yes, by other officers, and people from the DA's office," the witness said, supplementing the list.

"When you gave those answers to the detectives in 1989, it's the same answer you've given this jury today, isn't it?"

"Yes, I don't recall seeing the peephole."

"When you gave those statements to the police in 1989, you didn't know that anybody was making a claim against you in this case about the death of Sherman Griffiths, did you?"

"No, I didn't."

Sometimes you have to know when to quit with a witness.

"OK, were there any other occasions, other than the two times you went to collect the rent and get a key, that you went to the third-floor apartment after the door had been changed?" the landlord's lawyer asked, attempting to limit the number of opportunities Campbell had to observe the second hole.

"I know I had to go get the key. I probably had to go back two or three times to collect the rent, because I was given fifty dollars here, a hundred dollars there, that type of thing," Campbell answered while Burke visibly counted to five on the fingers of his right hand.

Lynch moved on to another topic.

"You saw the two-by-fours up there. Have you ever seen two-by-fours in a tenant apartment building before?"

"Yes, one of the tenants downstairs had them on his doors."

"There wasn't a doorknob on the door, do you recall that?"

"Yes, you just sort of put a key in, push it, and it would go in. I think I was a dead bolt lock. It's required for the Section 8 tenants."

"So each of the apartments at Bellevue Street had a different method of high security for keeping the door shut, would that be fair to say?"

"Yes, yes," Campbell agreed without hesitation.

"Now, Mr. Burke asked you about a drug arrest that took place in April of 1987. When was the first time you learned about the drug arrest?"

213

"It was at Mr. Burke's office, when Mr. Newman was deposing Bonnie Glenn. Attorney Newman produced the police report. It was the first time I had ever seen it. No one from the police or the building ever told me there had been a drug raid in April of 1987."

"Did any member of the Boston Police Department contact you to tell you that there was a drug problem at 102–104 Bellevue Street?"

"No. No one ever did."

"Did any tenant or anybody else ever complain that there was drug dealing going on at 102–104 Bellevue Street?"

"No, they did not."

"Mr. Burke asked you whether you cared where the rent money came from. What did you mean by your answer?"

"I answered his question 'I didn't care' because I don't go into people's personal business. I don't know if they are on welfare or social security. It wasn't really that much of a concern to me at the time."

"You had the right to interview tenants you were going to put into your apartment building, but you didn't have the right to do that with tenants who were already there, did you?"

"No, I couldn't."

"Mr. Campbell, would you tell the jury today whether you had any knowledge that anyone was dealing drugs at 102–104 Bellevue Street?"

"I had no knowledge at all."

"If you had such knowledge that that type of activity was going on at those premises, what would you have done?"

"I would have contacted the police."

"That's it, Your Honor. Thank you." Lynch smiled anxiously.

"Thank you, Mr. Campbell. You may step down. We'll take a short recess," Judge Butler told the jurors.

MICHAEL MCDONALD

When a party calls a witness to testify in a case, you are essentially vouching for the credibility and substance of his or her testimony. It creates a dilemma when the witness has beneficial information but is adversarial to your client's cause. If you don't put the witness on the stand, the jury will never learn important facts about the case. If you do call that person, the other side is free to cross-examine "your" witness.

"Good afternoon, Mr. McDonald," Her Honor said to ease the palpable tension.

"Good afternoon," the witness reciprocated in a barely audible response.

"Please keep your voice up loudly enough so that the jurors can hear your testimony," Judge Butler suggested politely as the plaintiff's lawyer stared at the witness.

"Would you state your name for the record, sir?" Burke asked after the man had been sworn.

"Michael McDonald."

This particular Michael McDonald never sang with the Doobie Brothers, and he certainly didn't have a mane of wavy gray hair. He was a second-rate electrician on loan from the loser's witness pool. A reluctant witness for the plaintiff, he was clearly aligned with Campbell and Bonnie Glenn. McDonald slunk into the witness seat and smirked at Burke.

"Where do you live?" the lawyer asked brusquely.

"Twenty-seven Canada Street, Lowell, Mass."

"Sir, are you here pursuant to the authority of a subpoena that was issued for your appearance to be here before today?"

The question did two things: it let the jury know it was necessary to subpoena McDonald to show up in court, and second, that he didn't appear when he was required to.

"Yes," the witness offered defensively.

"Did you honor that subpoena, sir?"

"No."

Burke knew that if he asked the witness why he didn't show up last Tuesday, there would be some lame excuse offered that McDonald had to bring his ailing mother for her chemo treatment or the parish priest needed some electrical work done at the bingo parlor. He chose to move on instead.

"Are you a friend of Mr. Campbell's?"

"Yeah, you know, business associate, friend," McDonald oozed in an attempt to limit the nature of the relationship.

"Well, he has paid you thousands of dollars to do repair work for him on the properties that he owns, hasn't he?"

"Yep."

"'Yep' means yes?" the lawyer responded sarcastically.

"Yes, sorry," the witness corrected himself, glancing sheepishly toward the jury enclosure.

"As a matter of fact you did repair work on Bellevue Street beginning in March of 1987, didn't you?" Burke asked, hoping the jury would make the connection to Detective Ruben Colon's arrest of a dealer at the same third floor apartment in April of the same year.

"I'm not sure of the exact date," the handyman fudged.

"Were you a licensed electrician at the time, sir?"

"No."

"When you performed the repair work you did for Mr. Campbell, did he personally accompany you to the location?"

"Yes."

"How many times have you been to Bellevue Street?"

"Several times."

"Several?" Burke mocked. "You've been in that apartment building over five hundred times, haven't you?"

"I can't say for sure," McDonald said softly as his upper body swayed side to side.

216

The questions that afternoon had been scripted after reviewing McDonald's deposition transcript. If the witness deviated from what he'd said previously, his prior statements could be used to refresh his memory or better yet impeach his credibility by showing he had said something different at another time.

"Do you recall being deposed, under oath, in my office?"

"Ah, no," the electrician fudged again.

Burke smiled and asked Her Honor for permission to approach the witness to show McDonald a copy of the thick deposition transcript of his previous testimony. Each page and line of the bound document was numbered in sequence for easy reference. Butler quickly nodded her approval. The jury wasn't exactly sure what was happening, but they knew it was something good.

"Do you recall being asked this question: 'Give me an approximation of how many times you went to Bellevue Street to do work?'"

"Uh-huh."

"Tell the jury what your answer was," the lawyer said as he pointed to the numbered line.

"A thousand times, five hundred easy," the witness answered without looking at the transcript.

"That's true, you'd been in that apartment building over five hundred times, hadn't you?"

"I guess," McDonald reluctantly agreed.

"Mr. Campbell accompanied you on a significant number of those occasions to Bellevue Street, didn't he?"

"Off and on," the electrician said, nodding.

"And you met Jimmy McConnell when you went there, didn't you? How would you describe Mr. McConnell?" Burke asked, holding the transcript in the air like an impending sledgehammer.

"Umm..." McDonald hesitated as small beads of sweat appeared at the edge of his hairline.

"Feel free, sir, just tell us how you described Mr. McConnell as when you saw him."

"A slouch, a weasel."

"Did Mr. McConnell offer to sell you drugs while you were present at Bellevue Street?"

The electrician knew by now there was no turning away from his previous deposition testimony.

"Yeah, cocaine," McDonald reluctantly admitted as he looked to the back of the courtroom. "It was in the basement and outside, a couple of different times," McDonald explained with a shrug of uncertainty.

"Did you ever have any interaction with the people up on the third floor?"

"No, not really. Well, yeah, I went up there, but the McConnells were the ones I dealt with the most."

"Didn't you say in your deposition that most of the people in that apartment building were quote 'dirtbags'?" Burke asked as he held the transcript up again for effect.

"Yeah."

"Did you notice the pedestrian traffic coming in and out of that apartment? People hanging around outside too?"

"There was always tons of people coming in and out of the building. There are six units. Coming and going all day long," McDonald added and then glanced anxiously at Campbell seated in the first row of the courtroom gallery.

"Do you recall being interviewed by Detective Reggie Rose from the Boston Police Department shortly after Sherman Griffiths was killed?" Burke asked as he shifted gears and produced a copy of the Boston police report of McDonald's interview.

For the briefest of moments the lawyer pictured Rose taking notes with a yellow legal pad and a matching number two yellow pencil, wondering if McDonald's questioning took place in the same room where Holly Robins had been interviewed with her father.

"Yes," the witness acknowledged after glancing at the account of his statement to Rose.

"Did you tell Detective Rose you were nervous whenever you were at Bellevue Street because drugs were being sold there?"

"Ah, I don't recall that exact statement," McDonald said, backtracking.

"Didn't you tell Detective Rose that people used to come to Jimmy McConnell's apartment, and McConnell used to go up the back stairway to the third floor and then return and the people would leave? You told him this would go on all day long, didn't you?"

"Yes."

"Sir, you knew there were a lot of drugs being sold there all day long, didn't you?"

"I don't know if there was a *lot* of drugs," McDonald said in a vain effort to limit the damage.

"When you saw this foot traffic going in there constantly all day long, Mr. Campbell was present on occasion too, wasn't he?"

"I'm not sure. I can't remember," the witness offered in a failed attempt to distance his friend from the scene.

"Do you have a memory of convenience?" the lawyer shot back, shaking his head in disbelief.

"No," McDonald responded without conviction.

"In fact, you were *more* concerned about the drug *users* coming in there than you were the drug *dealers* on the premises, weren't you?"

"Yes," the witness said as he squirmed uncomfortably.

"In fact, you were more concerned about the *drug buyers*, because you knew those were the kind of people that would cut your arm off with a Sawzall for a hundred bucks, right?"

"Objection," Lynch exclaimed as he rose to his feet, trying to break the flow.

"Overruled," Her Honor said sternly, turning to face the witness.

"Correct," McDonald nodded and slunk further into his chair.

Burke turned to his right as one of the jurors explained to two others that a Sawzall was a construction tool used to cut through just about anything made of wood or metal.

"It was obvious, right? Even to a casual observer, who was in and out of that apartment building, that there were drug users and drug dealers there, right?"

"Yeah," the electrician replied as he looked to the gallery again for support.

"You also knew that Shirley and James McConnell were drug users, because you had seen them on numerous occasions passed out on their couch at two o'clock in the afternoon, hadn't you?"

"Yes."

"None of these people worked, did they?"

"No."

"You told Detective Rose that Jimmy McConnell was always trying to impress you that he was the 'main man,' but, you knew he was too dumb to be the main man, didn't you? He was just a runner for whoever the real 'main man' was. He wasn't smart enough to be a drug dealer, was he?"

"Yes, I knew he wasn't no main drug dealer," McDonald explained cautiously.

"All the drugs were coming out of the third floor, weren't they?"

"Well, I guess you could speculate which apartment it was coming out of, ya know."

"And when you went up to that third-floor apartment, it looked like Fort Knox, didn't it?"

"Well, the guy had like two-by-fours on the door braced for a lock."

"And when you went inside the apartment, I'm sure you saw the reason that he had it barricaded so well, right? Because it was furnished so lavishly, wasn't it?" the lawyer asked derisively.

"No, it wasn't furnished lavishly at all," McDonald unwittingly countered.

"Would it be fair to characterize the interior of that apartment as a 'dump'?"

"Yes."

"Do you remember there being anything of value inside that apartment?"

"No. There was nothing of value in it. That's why I couldn't understand why the guy locked it up like he did."

There was a gaping, open-mouthed look from four of the jurors at McDonald's answer.

"There was nothing worth stealing in that place, was there?"

It was one of those moments when the electrician thought his answer wouldn't be so bad if he didn't have to say the words. He simply shook his head in response.

"You've got to say yes or no, verbally please," the lawyer instructed the witness.

"No," he whispered, passing barely over the threshold of hearing.

"Now Mr. Campbell came upstairs with you when you installed the intercom system, didn't he? Just about one week before Sherman Griffiths was shot and killed, wasn't it?"

"Yes."

"There was *another* hole directly below the peephole wasn't there?"

"Yes," McDonald acknowledged.

"Did you find anything else unusual about this door?"

"It had no doorknob."

"Did it strike you as unusual that you didn't see a doorknob on a door that was barricading the inside of a dump?"

"No. Nothing is unusual when you go down there, Dorchester. You just get used to it."

The lawyer paused briefly and turned to the jury to assess whether they accepted McDonald's evaluation of Dorchester. None of them offered an insight.

"Did you buy any drugs up there, sir?" the lawyer asked, waiting for an objection that never came.

"Yes, down there, on the first floor."

"I have nothing further," Burke announced as he paused for five seconds to stare at the witness and then took his seat.

*****

Lynch had his first question out before the jury could shift their eyes from the plaintiff's table.

"Mr. McDonald, how did you hear about the shooting?"

"I was watching the eleven o'clock news, and I called Tom up and I asked him, 'Did you see what happened at your building?'"

"What was Mr. Campbell's reaction?"

"Disgust. I think he was more—"

"Objection, Your Honor," Burke interjected.

"Sustained."

"Now, you received somewhere between five and ten thousand dollars for your work at Bellevue Street, right?" Lynch asked.

"Yes."

"When you were asked how many times you had been to Bellevue Street, were you trying to give the best answer you could how many times you had been there?"

"Yes, I can't possibly count how many times I was there."

Because the plaintiff called McDonald, Lynch was free to ask questions that suggested the answers to an already willing witness.

"You started working there in March and stopped sometime in 1987. How many working days in a year?"

"Three hundred and sixty-five minus holidays, two or three holidays," McDonald said.

"Aren't there somewhere in the vicinity of two hundred and fifty and three hundred working days in the year? You weren't there five hundred times, right?"

"No, probably not," McDonald readily agreed.

"And you expressed your opinion about the people living on Bellevue Street and in the Dorchester area as being 'dirtbags'?"

"Well, not so much a whole group of people, because there's good and bad. It's a dislike of people that just don't want to work and better themselves, you know? People like Mr. McConnell," the witness sneered.

"Did you ever share any of your observations about the tenants in the building with Tom Campbell?"

"Not to my recollection," McDonald said as he brought his hand up to scratch the top of his head.

"You didn't tell Mr. Campbell that you bought drugs at Bellevue Street, did you?"

"Definitely not. Tom wouldn't have gone for that at all. He would have had nothing to do with me. He'd be the last person I would tell."

"Your job would be history, so to speak?"

"From smoking a joint, I'd be all done with Tom."

"Now Mr. Burke asked you if purchased any drugs. What type was it?"

"I bought marijuana from Jimmy McConnell on the first floor."

"Mr. Campbell wasn't with you most of the time that you were on the premises, was he?"

"No, he'd come and show me what he wanted done, and he'd leave."

"And you expressed an opinion about the furnishings in the third-floor apartment. Were they consistent with other apartments in the building?"

"Very much so."

"You never observed a drug transaction, did you?"

"Not in front of me, no."

"You were asked if you saw a hole below the peephole. You didn't see one, did you?"

"Not that I recall, no."

"That's all," Lynch said with a sense of satisfaction.

Her Honor was quick to announce to the jurors that they were done for the day.

"We'll quit now at the conclusion of this witness and resume tomorrow at nine o'clock. Thank you very much. Have a good evening," she told them.

NORMAN BATES

As soon as Newman said the name, Burke knew the jurors all thought of Hitchcock's movie *Psycho*.

Norman Bates, the plaintiff's next witness, didn't look like actor Anthony Perkins. He didn't carry a long-bladed butcher knife, and he certainly didn't wear a wig or dress in his mother's clothes. His last name was Bates, but he didn't operate an anonymous motel on a deserted highway.

Norman Bates was an expert in the specialty of real estate management. He was there in courtroom 10 to testify about the reasonableness of Campbell and Glenn's management of their property on Bellevue Street. Before he was sworn in, Judge Butler gave the jury instructions on expert witnesses.

It was a teaching moment, and Her Honor was an excellent instructor.

"Most of the witnesses who have testified so far, if not all of them, have testified concerning what they, themselves, saw or did or experienced or heard. That is what is called direct testimony by a fact witness. It is the jury's task to assess those witnesses to determine whether the witness is reliable, someone to be believed on all or a portion of what they told you," Judge Butler explained as the jury nodded in acceptance.

"But there are also cases in which people are allowed to come in and give opinions. The basis for the opinion comes from the notion that there are some areas that may be beyond the general knowledge of jurors, lawyers, and judges, and require specialized knowledge. Often we will get medical experts in to testify about diagnosis, prognosis, or the causation of a particular disease. One of my colleagues actually had an expert testify about spider webs in a criminal case. The issue was to determine whether an entrance was made *in or out* of a window that was covered with spider webs." Her Honor smiled as the jurors got the point and returned the expression.

"Experts are allowed to give their opinions. Opinions meaning not necessarily what they saw, but drawing conclusions based upon what they have learned about the case or assumed facts to be true. But with respect to any witness, expert or fact, it is up to you to accept or reject any or all of their testimony. You determine the believability of any witness," the judge concluded, signaling the clerk to administer the oath to Bates.

A graduate of Northeastern University's criminal justice program with a law degree from Suffolk University, Norman Bates was the president of Liability Consultants, a firm providing advice on security-related issues to hotels, hospitals, and real estate companies across the country.

After eliciting his work and business addresses, Newman asked Bates to give the jury some background on his bona fides.

"We evaluate what their particular risks are and give clients recommendations on things they can do to improve security. Whether it's locks, fences, lighting, training their staff, focusing on crime and security issues specifically. We are also hired by both plaintiff and defense counsel to review cases and testify in court as an expert in our field."

"Approximately how many times have you testified as an expert in the Commonwealth of Massachusetts with respect to security issues, Mr. Bates?"

"Objection," Lynch said before the answer was given.

"Overruled," her Honor retorted before defense counsel could regain his seat.

"I'd say probably thirty to thirty-five times over the last ten years. Our caseload is fairly evenly split between plaintiffs and defense," Bates explained as he turned to the jury box.

As he listened to the witness's testimony, Burke could tell the jurors were interested, the first key to winning their acceptance and eventually their verdict.

"Can you explain to the jury what documents you reviewed in this case?"

"I read numerous depositions, trial transcripts, Boston police documents, photographs of the scene, and I actually inspected the door in question."

"What did you learn about the door on the third floor?"

"Objection," Lynch said in a half crouch out of his chair.

"Overruled," Her Honor responded softly.

"I was able to determine that this was a metal-clad door made by the Stanley Company. It was an exterior door, meant for the outside."

There were a series of other questions Bates was asked about his methodology before being asked his expert opinion. The jurors made no expression as several poised their pencils to write in their spiral notebooks.

"Based upon the materials you have reviewed, have you reached an opinion as to the reasonableness of the defendants' management of the 102–104 Bellevue Street building in Dorchester?"

"Objection, Your Honor," defense counsel tried again.

"Overruled," came the now familiar response.

"Yes, I do have an opinion. It breaks down into really two subject areas. First, according to the Boston police, there was a substantial history of crime in the neighborhood where the property was located. At least one of the defendants, Bonnie Glenn, was well aware of the drug problem in the area. In fact, there was a drug raid in the very same apartment less than twelve months before this incident," Bates offered as two of the jurors looked back to where the defendants were seated in the gallery.

Newman didn't interrupt the witness's train of thought.

"The apartment was occupied by several different people. Every time Mr. Campbell went to collect the rent in person, there was somebody different who paid the rent. The original tenant, Delray Ferguson, was never there. That, in my experience and opinion, was highly unusual," the witness continued as another juror joined in a search for an expression from Campbell and Glenn.

"There was also evidence of excessive amount of foot traffic, which is usually a pretty telltale sign of some illicit activity, specifically, drug trafficking activity. Shirley McConnell also stated that she told Campbell about the amount of nonstop foot traffic to the third floor, particularly in the evening hours."

Lynch had long since ceased objecting and joined the trio of jurors as he too took notes to use for his cross-examination.

"I think the more significant point is the existence of the metal-clad exterior door, which Mr. Campbell stated he was aware that it was there.

And that it was barricaded with two-by-fours and had no handle on the outside of the door. The door was totally dissimilar from any other door in the apartment building."

Bates was on a roll, in a hitter's groove. Like Yastrzemski at the plate sizing up a thigh-high fastball and with one swing, knocking it over the Green Monster.

"My opinion regarding the landlord's failures are in two parts: First, the landlords should have contacted the police department and relayed their suspicions, let them know about the flow of traffic and the different door being installed. Second, you just never allow a tenant to install their own door. This is the first time I had ever run into this in a case. I've seen situations where tenants want to add their own lock and get permission, but to allow a door like this is contrary to accepted practice anywhere in the country."

"Now the second hole beneath the peephole, is that an unusual item on a door?" Newman asked.

"Highly unusual, it's not something you'd ever see in a normal apartment door used day to day. It would allow you, as an outsider, to actually look into the apartment."

"I have no further questions for this witness," Newman said as he glanced toward the jury enclosure.

The anticipated request to see Judge Butler at the sidebar didn't take long.

"I'm making a motion to strike all of this witness's testimony," Lynch said out of the jurors' hearing.

"That motion is denied," Her Honor responded without fanfare, as plaintiff and defense counsel quickly exchanged places at the far end of the jury box.

THE EXPERT

As a lawyer, it's important to start and finish strong when conducting cross-examination of a witness. Frequently, with an expert, the intent is to call into question the assumptions made and the conclusions drawn from those assumed facts. It is also good to find some obscure comment made in another case and use it to contradict the person currently on the stand.

"Mr. Bates, you've testified in numerous premises liability cases, correct?" Lynch began with a wry smile.

"Yes."

"Let me read this quote to you: 'It's appalling to think that an innocent person could be held legally responsible for someone else's crime.' Do you know who the author of that statement is?"

"Yes."

"Who is it?" Lynch asked nonchalantly, tossing a ninety-five-mile-per-hour fastball high and tight at the witness in the box.

"It's a part of an opening line of an article that *I* wrote several years ago," Bates said softly as a twinge of red blush inched in an outward circle from the center of his cheeks.

Burke had to admire his thoroughness; Lynch had done his homework. Finding Bates's quote from some little-known seminar publication was like a magician pulling a white rabbit by its ears from a black top hat. The lawyers seated at the plaintiff's table exchanged a look of uncertainty with their expert witness as the cross continued.

"Now your opinion here is based on a number of factual assumptions about the testimony in this case, correct?"

"Yes, I assumed that the people who testified were under oath and telling the truth."

"You didn't hear any of those witnesses testify or look at them to judge their credibility during cross-examination, did you?" Lynch asked as he turned to the jury.

"Right."

"But if it's not true and credible, then your opinion fails, doesn't it?"

"Well, it may or may not. It depends on what it is."

"You read Bonnie Glenn's deposition in which she stated that she wasn't aware of any drug crime on Bellevue Street, didn't you?"

"Yes."

"You chose not to believe that though?"

"No. I didn't believe it or disbelieve it. I just said that she was aware of drug problems in Dorchester. That's what I testified to."

"Well, you're not saying landlords shouldn't have purchased a piece of property to rent to tenants or that every building in Dorchester's got a drug problem, are you?"

"No, I'm saying landlords should know what's going on in their building. There's a higher probability of drug activity in Dorchester than there would be in a town like Belmont."

"But you know there was only one instance of drug activity in that area before the raid of February of 1988 involving Officer Griffiths, correct?"

"Yes, in April of 1987," Bates said, without reminding the jury that the one instance was at the defendants' property.

"And you remember Mr. Campbell testifying in his deposition that he was unaware of the raid?"

"Yes."

"But you chose to disregard what he told you. You're deciding the credibility of witnesses then, aren't you?"

"Based on the bias that's inherently involved with Mr. Campbell being a party to the case, yes, I'd say that's a fair statement."

Lynch took a quick look at the laundry list of questions on his yellow notepad and forged ahead.

"You also said it was unusual that the apartment was occupied by several different people. Do you find it unusual, in an urban area like Dorchester, that there would be more than two people living there?"

"Well, taken by itself, it's not unusual. Any one of these things alone may not seem significant, but if you look at the cumulative effect, it paints a much different picture."

It was an effective cross-examination technique, taking each item mentioned by Bates individually and holding it up to scrutiny on its own merits.

"You don't find it unusual that the tenants pay their rent in cash, do you?"

"No."

"And as far as the foot traffic, Mrs. McConnell didn't tell Mr. Campbell why the people were knocking on her window. She told him the bell wasn't working and asked him to fix the problem, and he did, correct?" Lynch shrugged midquestion.

"Again, any one of these things standing alone does not appear to be significant. It's the cumulative..." Bates's voice trailed off.

"In your opinion, you also mentioned the metal-clad door. You would agree with me that the biggest problem in premises liability cases is crimes of violence committed on occupants? Landlords and occupants are worried about their security?"

"Yes," the expert readily agreed.

"And occupants have a right to take fair steps to protect their own personal security, correct?"

"Fair steps, yes."

"Economics is an issue too, isn't it? In terms of what some tenants can do personally to protect themselves, right? I mean you're not hired by the owners of these triple-deckers in Dorchester, are you?"

"No."

"That type of expertise and knowledge is something that's beyond their means, isn't it?"

"No, not necessarily. They could get the same advice for free from the crime prevention unit from the Boston Police Department, at least to know how to protect their properties with proper locks and doors."

You could tell by the scrunching of Lynch's nose that the unexpected answer didn't sit well with defense counsel.

"Now, a metal-clad door isn't an unusual thing to use inside for this type of building, is it?"

"Yes, it is. This type of door is not meant to be used in an interior setting," Bates countered.

"Well, the other door across the hall was metal-clad, too, wasn't it?" Lynch volleyed back.

"That's right."

"A tenant who replaces a door with a better door, you wouldn't tell the tenant that he did something wrong, would you?"

"Absolutely, it is totally contrary to accepted practice. You just don't do it. You've got to maintain control over that property. If a tenant puts in his own door and hardware, you lose that control. It doesn't make any sense at all."

"So if a tenant puts in his own door more secure than the previous one, you have a problem with that?"

"Yes, I do. First, the landlord doesn't have access to the apartment in an emergency, like a fire or medical emergency, and second, there is the potential damage to the property if the tenant does a lousy job installing it. Plus, there was the issue of the two-by-fours here."

By this time, the information was coming too quickly. The jury sat with their head pivoting from left to right, intently listening to each question and response echo across the invisible net in front of them.

"Mr. Campbell had no problem entering the apartment in this case, did he? When he needed to?"

"No, he didn't, but I've been in other apartments in Dorchester, and I've never seen two-by-fours being used. I've see police locks, but not two-by-fours."

"And you've referenced the fact that there's no door handle, but there's a dead bolt. You put the key in, you turn the dead bolt lock, and the door opens, correct?"

"Providing the two-by-fours aren't in place."

"So this is an aesthetic concern. There's no security improvement to having a doorknob, correct?"

"Yes."

"And you testified about the hole that was there?"

"Right."

"Your testimony is based on an assumption that the hole was there when Mr. Campbell had an opportunity to see it? That he would have noticed it, correct?"

"Yes, that he should have."

"But you don't know when the hole was installed?"

"No, we just know that it was done prior to the shooting."

"It could have been the day before or two days before—is that fair to say?"

"That's fair to say."

"So your whole criticism then, if we accept there were enough of these factors to raise a suspicion, is that the police should have been called, right?"

"Right."

"And you would expect that, if something illegal was going on in a building, that one of the tenants would tell you, wouldn't you?"

"You would hope so."

"But that didn't happen in this case, did it?" the landlord's attorney roared.

"Right," the witness reluctantly agreed.

"There's no witness in this case who said, 'I told Tom Campbell there was something wrong going on in that building,' is there?"

"Right," Bates said a second time as defense counsel turned his back and continued to his seat.

Burke hated to admit it, but Lynch had managed to tie the game in the bottom of the ninth. It was a full count as the pitch sailed toward the heart of the plate while the lawyers waited impatiently for the jurors to make their call.

DÉJÀ VU

Clerk Timilty asked the next witness to raise his right hand.

It was a familiar face, somehow positioned as a recurring witness from another case shared with the lawyer.

"Where are you employed?" Burke asked the detective with the dark, intense eyes.

"I've been a member of the Boston Police Department for the past twenty-five years. I'm currently assigned to the internal affairs division. Prior to that, I worked in the homicide unit for approximately seven years, investigating about two hundred and fifty cases. I was assigned there several months after Officer Griffiths died," Reggie Rose explained to the jury.

"Now did you at some point interview an individual by the name of Michael McDonald regarding the Griffiths case?"

The rules of civil procedure allow a party to introduce previous statements made by a witness that can then be offered to show that their testimony at trial is inconsistent with what they previously stated. Rose would perform that function regarding the testimony of the electrician working at Bellevue Street.

"Yes, I did a thirty-minute interview of Mr. McDonald at his home along with Sergeant Brendan Bradley and another detective from the homicide unit. He was initially very nervous and reluctant to speak to us or let us in his house."

"Can you tell the jury and the court what it is you recall about that conversation with Mr. McDonald?"

"Objection," Lynch said as he rose quickly from his seat in an attempt to curtail the inquiry.

"Overruled," Her Honor responded softly as she nodded for Rose to continue.

"Mr. McDonald related to us how he had been employed to install wiring and an intercom system at Bellevue Street in Dorchester. He related that he was very, very nervous working there. He said he had trouble getting into the third-floor apartment and would bang on the door, but couldn't gain entrance from the occupant, Albert Lewin. Finally, McDonald called Mr. Campbell, who responded and accompanied him to the third floor, and as a result, they were able to gain access to the apartment."

The jury sat impassively as Rose confirmed another layer of connection between Campbell and Lewin, placing the landlord inside the very apartment where the shots were fired that killed Sherman Griffiths.

"While inside, McDonald said he observed the door he had just gone through was secured by two-by-fours. He said the apartment was in disarray. It was a mess. He said he felt intimidated by Albert Lewin."

"Did he provide you with any other information?"

"Mr. McDonald said that while he was doing work there, he recalled a continuous flow of people coming to that address and meeting with Jimmy McConnell on the first floor, who would then go up the back stairs to Lewin's apartment and return with something, and then the people would leave. McDonald said there was continuous drug activity going on between McConnell and Lewin all day, every day that he was there."

"Did he indicate where the drugs were coming from?"

"The third-floor apartment, Mr. Lewin's apartment." Rose gestured upward.

"I have no further questions, Judge. Thank you," Burke announced as he turned back to take his seat.

*****

"Mr. Lynch?" Her Honor inquired.

Rose was a difficult witness to cross-examine. There were no errors or inconsistencies between his testimony and the written report of McDonald's interview. It would be interesting to see what the opposition would be able to do to weaken his testimony.

"Detective Rose, your presence in interviewing Mr. McDonald was to determine what he knew about the occupant of the third-floor apartment, correct?"

"I can't honestly say that was the reason, no," Rose countered.

"Well, didn't Captain Bradley, at the time Sergeant Bradley, tell you he was attempting to identify the person in the apartment?"

"No, Sergeant Bradley did not relate to me personally why or what we were doing there, other than we were going to interview somebody that had something to do with the death of Officer Griffiths. I was really kept at arm's length, so I did not know many of the intricate workings of the investigation."

"Well, you knew to ask him whether the gentleman on the third floor was Hispanic or not, didn't you?"

"I asked Mr. McDonald if he knew who that person was. First he identified Jimmy McConnell and then Albert Lewin, whom he said spoke with an accent as though he came from one of the islands. That was significant, I was told, because I guess they were trying to determine if Lewin did live up there. At the time, I knew about as much from the newspapers as I knew from the police department."

There was a brief pause as defense counsel examined the scribbled notes on his yellow legal pad.

"That's all the questions I have," Lynch said, dejectedly returning to his seat.

Judge Butler inquired to see if there was any redirect from the plaintiff's counsel, and when there was none, she excused Detective Rose from the stand.

She turned to the jury and made a brief announcement before dismissing them for the day.

"The lawyers report that the case is moving along faster than they anticipated. Chances are you will be getting it in your hands no later than Wednesday and possibly as early as Tuesday. I'm going to stop now and send you home a little early. So please, don't talk about the case. I don't know if there will be any reports on the television or the radio or newspaper about this case. If there are, you are instructed not to see, not to view, not to listen to, and not to read any of the reports if there are any. I'll see you Monday morning at nine o'clock. Thank you."

DEIRDRE GRIFFITHS

Dee was the first witness to take the stand on the Monday morning after the weekend. The summer wind had shifted, bringing with it a chilly start to the new day. It was just after nine in the morning when Judge Butler asked the jurors the usual questions about whether they had read anything about the case.

None had.

"Good morning, Mrs. Griffiths." Her Honor smiled as the plaintiff responded in kind and raised her right hand.

Burke was careful not to refer to the witness by her first name in his opening question. The courtroom was still as Dee told the jury about her education at Mercy Nursing School in Maryland and then her work experience at Children's Hospital, where she first met her future husband.

"What kind of work did Sherman do at Children's?" Burke asked, momentarily reminded of Ruth.

"When we met he was in an intern program for pharmacy. At the time he was delivering medications to the floors and taking calls on the poison control phone, but he had always wanted to become a police officer."

"Can you describe him for us physically?"

"Sherm was six-foot-one, about two hundred and twenty pounds. He had reddish hair, a big full beard. He was boisterous, happy, very lively, and very friendly. We dated for two years and were married in June 1981."

"Did you have any children?" Burke asked, and Dee nodded.

"Yes, we have two girls. Hillary is thirteen now, and Melanie is twelve. Hillary was born eleven months after we were married, and Melanie was born thirteen months after Hillary. The girls were six and five years old when—"

239

Burke realized that Dee was becoming upset at the mention of Sherm and the two girls and gently broke in to ask. "Where did you live when you were first married?"

"We lived in Dorchester, in Savin Hill."

"Can you tell the jury where Sherman worked after he left Children's Hospital and joined the Boston police?"

"After completing the academy, he was assigned to Dorchester, then Roxbury, West Roxbury, and I think it's called Area A in downtown Boston. He took Spanish classes to help deal with the Spanish-speaking community. Then he was assigned to the drug unit."

The questions up to that point were intended to provide the jury with a snapshot of his client's life and marriage, but there was no easy way to approach the topic of death, no perfectly phrased question to ask.

"When did you first learn that Sherman had died?"

"It was the evening of February 17. I was at home doing my coupons for food shopping when one of Sherm's brothers called and told me that, that..."

Somehow, Dee never quite got the rest of the words to the sentence out. Things went deathly quiet in the courtroom as the witness bit her lip to stop from crying. She stiffened her posture in the chair and slowly continued.

"You see, we had moved. The Boston police still had our old Dorchester address, and they were having a hard time finding me," she told the courtroom in a voice that cracked and ebbed into a soft murmur.

Time had failed to erase her memory of loss. Some of the jurors closed their eyes, and others turned away to look down at their folded hands.

"Can you describe your relationship with Sherman before he died?"

"We had an excellent relationship. It's hard to explain in words. He was the love of my life." Dee smiled weakly. "He was the only one, and probably will be the only one that...that I've ever shared that kind of closeness with."

"Since 1988, have you dated anyone?"

"No."

"Do you have a social life?"

"Well, with my children. I do a lot of chauffeuring. I have some friends I go out to lunch with."

"You talked about your relationship. Can you tell us some of the things that you did with him that you cannot do now?"

"Much of our relationship revolved around just daily life. Waking up together, reading the paper, having somebody who appreciated eating the food I prepared. Someone to share the parenting duties with, taking care of the house, and just sharing hopes and dreams for the future. We had so many plans. Sherm wanted to go back to school and become a lawyer."

For some reason, Burke thought of Charlie Dunn, the loss of his first wife and his return to the law.

"How was he as a father?"

"He was a really good father. He planned and went on field trips at school with the girls. I think, because his father had died when he was eight, Sherm really wanted to see that they had what he had missed. He took the girls on field trips to Plymoth Plantation, the Museum of Science in Boston, and the Blue Hills to the Boston Police Mounted Unit so they could ride the horses there. That was his idea. He loved it."

"Do you have any photographs that represent the type of relationship you and the girls had with Sherm?"

"Has defense counsel seen these photos, Mr. Burke?" Judge Butler asked.

"Yes, Your Honor," Lynch agreed quickly.

So the moments captured of a life together in ten photographs were introduced and circulated among the jurors; they carefully held the pictures of the couple's wedding day, on a boat deep-sea fishing, Sherm's graduation from the police academy, the smiling father holding the girls after their births, vacations on Cape Cod making sand castles, family camping trips to New Hampshire, the girls' baptisms. They were all there for the viewing of a life together, and then nothing.

"You told us about learning that Sherman had been shot and killed. Can you tell the jurors how your life has changed since then?"

"We really had a good marriage. It's just a totally different life now. I don't have someone who does...who shares my concerns and who shares my life the way that he did," Deirdre explained, holding the moment of loss.

"Did you love Sherman?"

"Very much," the widow said as she brought her clasped hands toward her and dropped her chin to her chest.

"Thank you, Judge. No further questions."

"Mr. Lynch?" Her Honor asked as she motioned with her hand toward the witness.

"Thank you, Mrs. Griffiths. We don't have any questions for you."

"We rest, Your Honor," Deirdre and Sherm's lawyers told Judge Butler.

JOHN ARNSTEIN

Detective John Arnstein had been assigned to Dorchester's Area C for over twenty-five years. He would be a brief first witness for the defendants, called to the stand to rebut and undermine the testimony of Rodney Black.

"What was the purpose of your interview with Mr. Black?" Lynch began.

"To see if Mr. Black could identify the person who shot him and determine if he intended to prosecute that person," Arnstein explained without emotion.

"With respect to your interview, did you ask Mr. Black any questions about his involvement with 102–104 Bellevue Street?"

"Yes, we were attempting to find out if he knew why he got shot. Mr. Black told us he had stolen some drugs from that building."

"Did he tell you whether he had any other involvement with that location, other than that one incident in which he stole the drugs?"

"He knew about the place. I don't know if Mr. Black actually told me if he had any other more involvement with it."

Stymied for the moment, Lynch pulled out a copy of Arnstein's previous deposition transcript to "refresh his memory" about the area of inquiry.

"Do you recall being asked this question in your deposition? 'Did Black tell you what, if any, involvement he had with the drug dealing at Bellevue Street?'"

"Yes, Black said that he had none," the detective agreed, acknowledging Black had not told the entire truth during the interview.

"Detective, did you ever tell the landlord at 102–104 Bellevue Street that the individual who shot Mr. Black had been arrested for this incident?"

"Did I? No, I didn't."

"Thank you, sir. Thank you. That's all the questions I have," defense counsel said as he turned to survey the jury.

ROBERT RUSSO

Bob Russo was an expert witness called by the defense. Russo was an experienced Boston legal whiz who specialized in the fine art of tenant evictions. He was a pleasant-appearing and knowledgeable lawyer intended to offset the impact of the plaintiff's expert Norman Bates. His testimony would contradict the conclusions reached by Bates, providing the jury with another frame of reference.

"Good morning, sir, can you tell me what you do for a living?"

"I'm an attorney with a practice in landlord and tenant law. I have represented landlords for the past eighteen years, appearing primarily in the Boston Housing Court," Russo explained to the attentive jurors.

"Are you familiar with the landlord tenant laws?"

"Yes, I am." Russo nodded as he turned to the jury and then to Burke. It was the look of well-earned superiority, given by those who knew their business and welcomed a challenge from someone operating outside the realm of the Boston Housing Court.

Lynch quickly cut to the chase.

"Now, can you tell me whether a landlord in Boston can evict a tenant without a reason?"

"No." The defendant's expert said with certainty.

"Now are you familiar with 102–104 Bellevue Street?"

"Yes, I am."

"So, at the time of this incident, could a landlord evict a tenant there on Bellevue Street for no reason?"

"No, there would have to be a legitimate reason. The standard reason, of course, is nonpayment of rents. But other grounds are nuisance, criminal activities, breach of quiet enjoyment, and interference with other tenants' use of their apartment."

"What are the procedures available to a landlord to evict a tenant for drug dealing?" Lynch asked.

"Depending on the facts, the first is under MGL chapter 139, section 19. You would need to have a Boston police incident report, which would identify the property in question, the officers involved, if any drugs were found, and whether or not it was actually a controlled substance. The state lab analyzes whatever was found in the unit to make sure it's an illegal drug.

"If the test is positive, a landlord can file for an injunction in the Boston Housing Court naming the tenant as a defendant. At the hearing, I would subpoena the arresting officer to show that he was present at the scene where the drugs were found and have him bring a certified copy of the drug analysis from the crime lab.

"If the analysis was positive, we would have a trial or make an attempt to mediate with the tenant and make sure they would leave on a certain date. Of course if the analysis came back negative, I would dismiss the case."

"Now you've had experience in attempting to evict tenants for drug dealing?" Lynch asked.

"Yes, I would say about fifty times," Russo responded as he turned toward the jury box.

"OK. If you had a landlord for a client who came to you and wanted to evict a tenant, but he didn't have an arresting officer and a drug analysis certifying that the substance seized was illegal, would you bring that case?"

"No, you don't have the evidence to go forward. I wouldn't waste a court's time or my client's money."

"Now, assume that a landlord reported to you that a tenant had installed a metal-type door and secured it with two-by-fours, there was a hole in the door, and there was a lot of foot traffic the landlord noticed going into the building and to the apartment. Would you use that evidence in support of an eviction procedure?"

"No, I would not. All that shows is that a door was installed. It doesn't lead me to the conclusion that drugs were or could be found in the apartment. I would need a positive drug analysis from the state lab."

"Thank you, sir. That's all the questions I have," Lynch concluded quickly.

MCLE

There was tension in the courtroom as the lawyer seated in the witness chair and the one at the far end of the jury enclosure sized the other up. Like two stray dogs meeting for the first time, their eyes narrowed and pupils dilated, each in search of a measure of dominance.

"Just so I understand you, sir, if you didn't have a drug analysis you wouldn't bring that type of eviction case?" Burke began slowly.

"That's correct."

"Do you recognize the book I'm holding in my hand?"

"It's an MCLE book. It stands for Massachusetts Continuing Legal Education. It's a book for lawyers to further their education in the legal field."

"Do you have this volume, the *Basic Practice Manual?*"

"No. I do not have that specific volume," Russo responded evenly.

"As a practicing attorney with some eighteen years experience, do you continue to keep updated in the area you have an expertise in?"

"That's correct."

"But you've never read this? The *Basic Practice Manual?*"

"Objection," Lynch said, attempting to break the flow.

"Overruled," Her Honor announced.

"That volume? No."

"And so you wouldn't know, sir, how this particular volume suggests one deals with just the type of situation you're talking about?"

"You'd have to tell me what date the book was printed."

"Last year." Burke smiled, cutting off an escape route.

"Um-hmm. No," Russo responded.

"Would you agree, sir, that if a landlord believes that a violation of chapter 139 is occurring in the unit, that he or she should contact the police so that they can investigate? Would you agree with that?"

"Yes, I would."

"And the statute you mentioned before, it doesn't actually *require* you to find drugs in the unit to evict a tenant, does it?"

"Correct."

"Would you also agree, sir, that once the landlord calls the police, they can also determine if they have made any other arrests there and get a copy of that police report? Would you agree with that?"

"Yes, sir." Russo nodded.

"Did you know Mr. Campbell took possession of 102 Bellevue Street on March 12, 1987?"

"Sounds like it was around then."

"So if Mr. Campbell had come to you as his attorney and said, 'I haven't found any drugs, but I have reason to believe they're dealing drugs out of one of my apartments,' you would agree there is a means to determine if there were any police reports on file?"

"Yes."

"OK. So if Campbell had come to you a month after he had taken possession of Bellevue Street and said, 'I think my tenants are dealing drugs,' you would have been able to find this particular police report dated April 2, 1987, regarding the very same apartment unit in his building, wouldn't you?"

"Probably," the eviction attorney said, shifting uncomfortably.

"Have you read this report, sir?" Burke asked as he approached the stand.

"No."

"Let's take a few seconds to read it, if you would. May he do that, Judge?"

"Yes," Her Honor answered as she reviewed her own copy of the document describing Ruben Colon's search of the third floor at Bellevue Street.

The room went still as both the judge and witness read the document and looked up simultaneously for the next question.

"This police report indicates that they took a loaded, a fully loaded .38-caliber pistol out of the same third-floor unit in Mr. Campbell's building on April 2, doesn't it?"

"Yes," Russo agreed.

"Does it indicate they also took twenty-two packets of cocaine from inside there too?"

"They took it out of the pants of a suspected drug runner, yes."

"Sir, do you believe the information contained in this police report would have been sufficient for a housing court judge to remove the tenants from that particular apartment?"

"I can't say with certainty; maybe not."

"Maybe yes, though, right?"

"That's correct."

"It's certainly worth a try, isn't it?"

"Absolutely."

"Do you agree that the landlord *must* take action, otherwise he or she may be subject to state and federal forfeiture of their property, and they can be subject to a civil suit by other tenants or parties who are lawfully on the premises and are injured by drug dealers?"

"Yes, I do agree. That's correct."

"Have *you* ever been to 102–104 Bellevue Street?"

"No, I haven't."

"I show you exhibit ten: it's a photograph of the door to this unit. Have you *ever* seen any holes like that underneath the peephole?"

"No."

"Sir, based on your eighteen years of experience, if a client comes to you and he says, 'I've got a tenant that I've never met. They've got no visible means of support. Every time I go up there, there's always somebody different up there, they tell me it's a cousin, or a brother. They always pay me in cash. Sometimes part of it in the morning, then I come back in the afternoon and they pay the rest. I don't know where they get their money. They got no jobs that I can see. One time a big guy shows up with a lot of gold chains and a big wad of cash and gives my business partner four hundred dollars for the rent.'"

Burke turned to face the jury before continuing with his hypothetical question.

"Your client tells you, 'I also found out the police raided their apartment three weeks after I bought it and found a loaded .38-caliber pistol and twenty-two packets of cocaine. The place itself is a dump, there's no heat, but they've got it barricaded like Fort Knox. There's nothing worth stealing up there, just some snow tires, an old couch, and a black-and-white TV.'

"The client tells you more. He says, 'The other day one of my tenants tells me there's a lot of foot traffic coming in and out all the time. And the other day I was up there and they put in this new steel door. It's an exterior door. It's got no doorknob, but it's got a little peephole and another hole drilled out underneath the peephole. They did this without my knowledge or my permission.'

"After that your client tells you, 'My electrician, who's been up there, and he doesn't even have a college degree, but he tells me he thinks they're all drug dealers. He's seen them at two o'clock in the afternoon passed out in their bedrooms. He says they're all dirtbags, drug dealers, and users, the kind of people who would cut your arm off with a Sawzall for a hundred-dollar bill.'

"Now, your client tells you all that information. Don't you think you've got a basis to initiate a complaint in the Boston Housing Court?" Burke exhaled quickly and turned back to face the witness.

"I would tell my client to contact the police department first."

"Yes, you'd tell him to do that, wouldn't you?"

"Absolutely."

"Don't wait around for some disaster to happen?"

"No."

"For some innocent party to come up there and get shot in the head and die as a result—"

"Objection," Lynch said, trying to stop the train.

"—in a building that you own."

"Sustained," Her Honor ruled.

"Thank you, Judge. That's all I have for this witness."

"Yes," Butler replied as Burke turned away from the jury and carefully placed the MCLE manual on the table in front of his seat.

THE VERDICT

September 12 was a picture-perfect, seventy-two-degree day, with an azure sky and the hint of autumn carried on a light breeze. Both sides had exhausted their list of witnesses in the previous six days of trial, relegated now to their final arguments, the judge's instructions on the law, and of course, the jury's verdict.

Black's Law Dictionary is the most frequently cited legal reference source in the country. It defines the word *verdict* as originating from the Latin phrase *veredictum*, meaning "to speak the truth."

Courtroom 10 that morning was filled with family, friends, and supporters from both sides, anxious and tense, uncertain how the day would unfold. Her Honor called the parties to the sidebar, asking whether they wanted all fourteen jurors to deliberate or have two removed by lottery. The decision was made to keep all fourteen. Unlike a criminal case where the verdict must be unanimous, a civil suit requires five-sixths of those deliberating, or twelve of the fourteen jurors, to agree.

The entire panel smiled in unison when the judge informed them they all would take part in deciding the case.

"This is essentially a negligence action, and the question is whether or not the landowners, Thomas Campbell and Bonnie Glenn, exercised due care to guard against reasonably *foreseeable* harm to people who would be lawfully on those premises," Her Honor began in a brief explanation of the controlling issue before the jury.

"If that question is answered affirmatively, then, of course, the issue would be what is a fair and reasonable compensation award to provide for the family of Sherman Griffiths, if there was negligence that caused his death?"

Butler would later explain the meaning of the words *negligence, foreseeable*, and *proximate cause* to the jury in much greater detail following counsels' closing arguments.

Because the plaintiff has the burden of proof in a civil case, they argue to the jury last. The defense lawyers for the two landlords each took their turn, dividing their allotted time to speak on behalf of each defendant, with Smith going first for Bonnie Glenn, followed by Lynch for Thomas Campbell. Although present for each day of the trial, Bonnie Glenn's role in the case was secondary to that of Thomas Campbell. Campbell had been physically present at Bellevue Street and had personal interaction with the tenants on the third floor. The argument on Glenn's behalf was brief, allowing for more of the defense's allotted time to be used by Frank Lynch.

It was a solid presentation of the defense's view of the evidence, highlighted by Campbell and Glenn's efforts to improve the Bellevue Street property and the failure of the police, or any tenant, to notify the landlords of drug dealing. The defense attorneys focused on the quote from the plaintiff's expert Norman Bates, arguing it would be "appalling" to hold a property owner responsible for the criminal acts of a drug dealer. They argued that everything seems clearer in hindsight, questioning the motives of some of the plaintiff's witnesses. In the end, they concluded, it was clear Campbell had cooperated with police, consistently telling the same story before and after the lawsuit: he never saw the second hole beneath the peephole and was unaware of any illegal activity of his tenants.

When he was finished, Frank Lynch thanked the jury and asked them to return their verdict in favor of the defendants.

Newman and Burke had quietly debated who should make the closing argument on behalf of their client. Each wanted the final opportunity to convey their emotional connection to a case that meant so much to both of them.

"I need to do this for my father," Newman told Burke. "He always tried to help the people in Chelsea where I grew up. I want to do the same thing here."

Newman began by saying it was a case of holding the defendants to an objective, legal, and social standard of what we expect from reasonable landlords. He spoke of the courage of Officers Colon and Schroeder, describing the first entry by Colon through the original wooden door without the two-by-fours, and months later, the subsequent inability to take down the reinforced door with the battering ram, resulting in the death of Griffiths. Newman questioned the dubious claim by Campbell that he never saw the second drilled pass-through hole despite numerous occasions at the scene prior to the shooting.

Newman spoke of an insider's view into the scene of a drug house, provided by Campbell's property "caretaker" Shirley McConnell and Rodney Black. He argued it should have been clear to even the most casual observer that the reinforced door and the second hole facilitated a large-scale drug operation that took over not only the tenants in the building but the area surrounding Bellevue Street as well. He spoke of the constant flow of foot traffic, the lack of heat in the apartment, multiple payments of rent in cash, no visible means of support for the unidentified tenants, the sparse furnishings with a state-of-the-art intercom system, and the steel door with no doorknob.

Just before he finished, Newman turned to the gallery, gestured to his client, and then said to the jury, "We entrust this case to you."

Judge Butler thanked counsel for their presentation of the case before beginning her instructions on the law. It was a teaching moment, intended to balance the rights and obligations of the parties. Her Honor used a chalkboard to write out the terms she would later define. The jurors had grown accustomed to her easy manner and turned warmly to listen as she summarized the logic and letter of the law.

The woman in the black robe explained that the owner of land has a *duty* to maintain his or her property in a reasonably safe condition; while a landlord is not a guarantor of the safety of the persons in the building, a landlord is not free to ignore reasonably foreseeable risks of harm to people who are lawfully on the premises.

Negligence is the breach of a duty owed by a defendant to another person, she detailed as the collection of citizens listened intently. It is a lack of diligence or a failure to do what the ordinarily careful person would do.

The court told the fourteen jurors they should consider any evidence that the landlords either *actually knew*, or *should have known*, that a shooting might occur in the building. Should one or both of the two landlords have been aware of information to cause a reasonably prudent landlord to conclude that drug activities were going on?

She cautioned them that even if there was negligence, or a breach of the landlord's duty, the plaintiff must then prove the breach of duty was a substantial contributing cause of the death of Sherman Griffiths. The burden of proof is always on the plaintiff. It's not enough to simply show there was negligence on the part of the defendants; the negligence must have been the proximate cause of the death of Sherman Griffiths.

When Butler was finished, the jury was escorted by two court officers past the crowded gallery to the nearby deliberation room.

They wouldn't be there long.

"Mr. Foreman, have you and twelve of your members reached a verdict?" Her Honor asked the assembled group shortly past the lunch hour.

"Yes, we have, Your Honor," the anxious man responded as he handed the verdict slip over to the court officer, who passed it to the clerk, who delivered it to Judge Butler.

AFTERMATH

One week after the jury's verdict on the Griffiths case, the *Boston Globe* printed an editorial roundly criticizing the conclusions reached by the fourteen members of the panel who had listened to six days of testimony. No reporter for the *Globe* was ever present for any portion of the trial. No one from the editorial staff ever heard any witness testify, interviewed any of the lawyers or parties to the case, or reviewed any transcript of the proceedings.

Despite their absence, the *Globe* suggested the verdict unfairly penalized the landlords and misdirected society's anger for Lewin's acquittal. The editorial read as follows:

> *A jury awarded Griffiths' widow more than a million dollars on the grounds that the two landlords should have known that drug dealing was going on in an apartment on Bellevue Street in Dorchester in 1988. One of the landlords visited the building regularly, received the rent in cash from several different young men, and, the plaintiff argued, must have noticed that a metal reinforced door had been installed with a small hole in the middle to dispense drugs. Cash is legal tender for "all debts public and private," and it is not reasonable to presume that all young men are criminals. A metal-clad door is a common security device, and the landlords say they did not notice the hole…They are thinking of appealing, but if they do not, the money will be paid out of a liability policy. The premium is paid by landlords from rents they receive each month. If this verdict is sustained, innocent tenants might have their rents raised to pay for a jury's misguided search for justice.*

The landlords of Bellevue Street did appeal the verdict against them to the state's highest court.

In a decision written by Judge Ruth Abrams, the Supreme Judicial Court held it was not "foreseeable" that Sherman Griffiths would be shot at Bellevue Street. In its recitation of the evidence, the court ignored the testimony regarding the amount of foot traffic to the third floor and the use of the pass-through hole, choosing to refer to it as a second "peephole" and the attempted drug rip-offs as "break-ins" that somehow justified the tenants' replacement of the existing door with a more secure metal-clad door.

In the statement of facts, considered by the court in the "light most favorable to the plaintiff," the justices concluded that the prior police drug raid on the same third-floor apartment was insufficient to put Campbell on notice that drugs were being sold on his premises. The seizure of the .38-caliber handgun and twenty-two packets of cocaine were nonfactors in the eyes of the court. The SJC also ruled there was no increased risk to the officers by the delay in their ability to take down the steel door reinforced by the two-by-fours, and nothing the landlords did, or failed to do, contributed to or created a risk of harm to people who were lawfully present there.

The Supreme Judicial Court overturned the verdict against the Bellevue Street landlords, finding them not responsible and reversing the jury's verdict.

It was a bitter ruling.

"I could accept their decision if I thought for a moment it was intellectually honest, but it wasn't," Newman said as the pair dejectedly sat reading the notice in their office.

"I think the court's ruling was a carryover from the police misconduct in Albert Lewin's criminal case," Burke said. "This verdict became a societal issue because it shifted more responsibility to property owners. There was no way the SJC was going to ever allow this case to succeed. They just weren't going to let that happen."

Deirdre was stoic when she met with her attorneys; she had grown accustomed to the slights that her life afforded. In her mind, she had fulfilled her responsibility to Sherman by bringing the suit. She didn't need the appellate court's approval of the jury's decision to know in her heart what was right.

It was different for her lawyers.

There were days after the ruling when Burke sat alone in the silence of his office, without the music playing. He refused to take any calls, reading the decision over and over until it was memorized. For the first time in his career, he lost all sense of trust and belief in the very system designed to instill confidence that the truth will win over anything else. The lawyer began to doubt not just the institutions of law, but he came to doubt himself. Devastated by the loss, he was adrift, without a sense of purpose, a failure.

I was a fool to believe, Burke told himself in a seemingly endless period of misgiving and uncertainty.

THE GIFT

It was early autumn, and a full moon cast a pale shadow in the warm night air. Burke took a familiar seat at the mahogany bar inside Crickets, ordered the usual, and for some reason began to think of the frail black woman. Her memory beckoned from their journey together, undimmed by the passage of time.

Curious, after all these years he could remember so clearly the first and the last time he ever saw Ruth.

The lawyer closed his eyes, recalling the moment, years ago, when he entered her hospital room and the sense of loss he felt.

In his mind, he could see Ruth wrapped in white linen sheets with her bare arms draped on each side of her thin body and still hear her last words to him as he stood next to her bed.

"Never lose the chance to help someone, to do what is right for them. Even if helping someone hurts you in the end, you need to give your love, your gift, to others," the dying woman told him.

Burke hated the place that Ruth's memory brought him, the place where he couldn't speak. The place where his throat closed in on him and his eyes began to well with tears. He fought it, but wanted, needed, to hear her words so desperately at that moment.

They had remained etched in his mind.

"I think God had you give me the gift that *I* needed back then. I never told you this, Timmy, but that day you took my case, the day you said you would help me, I left your office and went outside. It was the first time since my Lonnie died that I heard the birds sing."

Burke could still see Ruth's face as she closed her eyes and softly whispered, "You gave me hope."

The lawyer smiled for the first time in weeks at the thought of Ruth's words, her final gift to him. He pushed the unfinished drink away and caught his reflection in the mirror behind the mahogany bar as he headed out the door.

Overhead, a silent flock of Canada geese were silhouetted in the moon-lit October sky over Boston.

"Maybe the Red Sox will win it all next year," he said aloud to no one in particular.

EPILOGUE

In October of 2004, the Boston Red Sox won their first World Series title in 86 years.

Shortly after his acquittal, Detective Alton Frost was shot in the buttock during an attempted arrest of a drug suspect. He retired on a disability from the Boston Police Department. His assailant was never apprehended.

The drug charges against Larry Goldman were ultimately dismissed. The Prince of the City was subsequently indicted two years later for conspiracy to murder a former Boston police officer named John Glenn.

Antonio Gomes was convicted of three counts of first-degree murder for the deaths of Basilisa Melendez and her two children, Johanna and Kenneth. Gomes was given three consecutive life sentences by Judge James P. Donohue and remains incarcerated at the Massachusetts correctional facility at Norfolk, Massachusetts. He has no parole eligibility date.

Michael Quarto and David Giacalone were convicted for the kidnapping and rape of the "water baby," Ginnie Freeman. They were sentenced to forty to sixty years in state prison. In March 2005, Giacalone was released on parole. Quarto became eligible for parole in 2009.

On March 13, 1986, a jury convicted Louis Pina on three counts of aggravated rape. He was given a sentence of twenty-seven to forty years in prison. Pina became eligible for parole in 2009.

Reggie Rose retired after more than thirty years of dedicated service to the City of Boston. He spent ten years in the homicide unit and investigated over a thousand felonies. If asked, Rose will tell you the most significant case in his career was the rape of Holly Robins.

Charlie Dunn remains in active practice with his son and nephew, representing doctors and hospitals throughout the Commonwealth of Massachusetts.

Deirdre Griffiths is the successful mother of two daughters, Hillary and Melanie. She resides in a suburb of Boston and works as a pediatric care nurse.

Following their successful appeal to the Supreme Judicial Court, Frank Lynch and William Smith, the two attorneys for the landlords, were chosen as "Lawyers of the Year" for their defense of the Sherman Griffiths case.

Elizabeth Butler retired after thirteen years as a trial judge. She currently works as a private arbitrator.

Mark Newman left the practice of law and was appointed as a juvenile court judge in the Lawrence District Court.

My friend Ruth died of heart failure on a sunny day in June. She is buried not far from a broad maple tree and is frequently serenaded by the passing birds above.

I miss her.

Made in the USA
Middletown, DE
22 June 2017